United States Department of Agriculture

I0439823

Use of Ancillary Data to Improve the Analysis of Forest Health Indicators

David Gartner, Editor

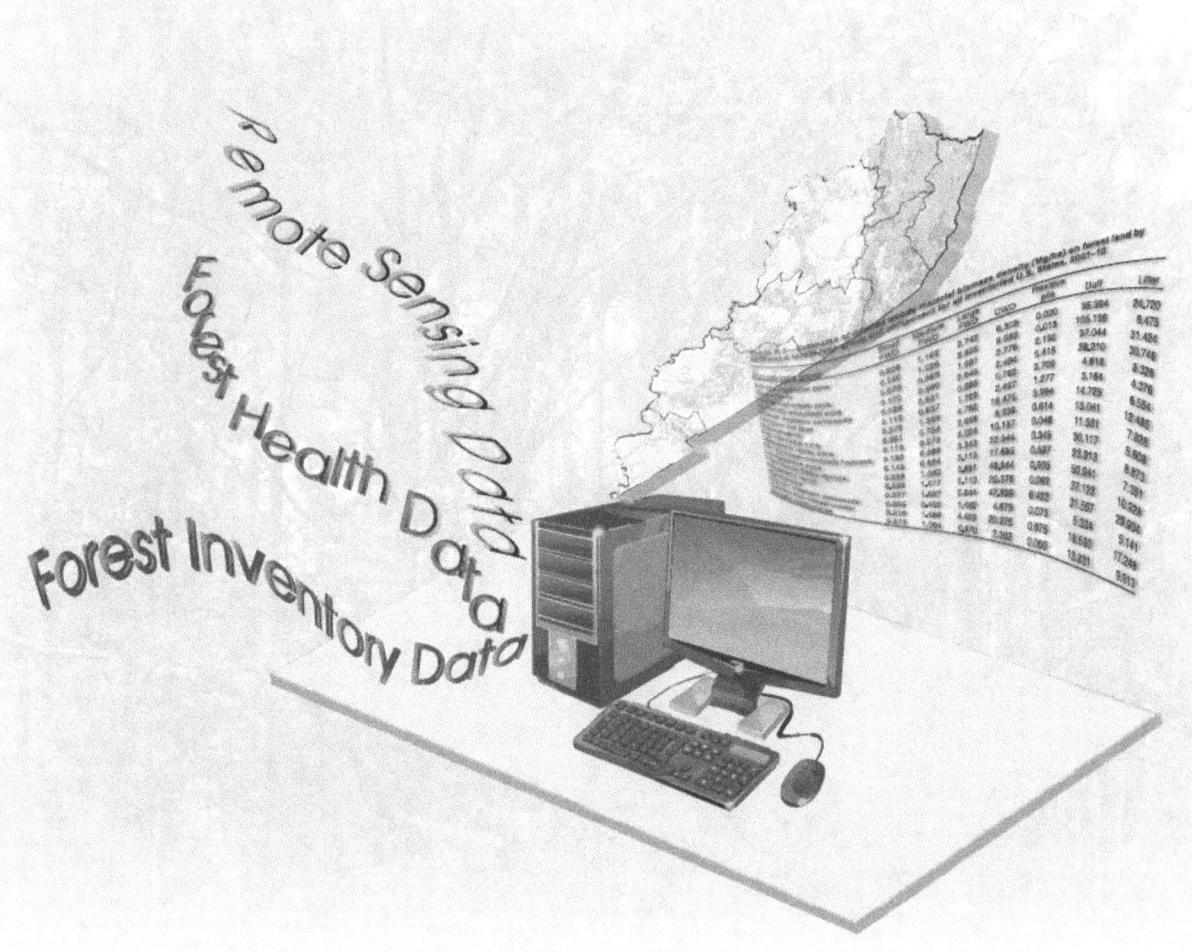

Southern Research Station

Author

David Gartner, Mathmatical Statistician,
U.S. Department of Agriculture Forest
Service, Southern Research Station,
Knoxville, TN 37919.

Cover artwork: Janet Griffin

www.srs.fs.usda.gov

July 2013

Southern Research Station
200 W.T. Weaver Blvd.
Asheville, NC 28804

Use of Ancillary Data to Improve the Analysis of Forest Health Indicators

David Gartner, Editor

Contents

Abstract

In addition to its standard suite of mensuration variables, the Forest Inventory and Analysis (FIA) program of the U.S. Forest Service also collects data on forest health variables formerly measured by the Forest Health Monitoring program. FIA obtains forest health information on a subset of the base sample plots. Due to the sample size differences, the two sets of variables have traditionally been analyzed separately. However, the analysis of forest health indicator data can occur in conjunction with not only other stand characteristics (mensuration variables such as live-tree volume), but also with a plethora of ancillary information such as climate data and satellite imagery. This document is designed to help people interested in using auxiliary information in the analysis of the forest health indicators. Readers are initially treated to topics related to exploratory data analysis. This introductory content is followed by presentation of various statistical methodologies that may be employed; each section provides empirical analyses and discussion of the technique being presented. To cultivate a common theme throughout the document, carbon attributes of coarse woody debris (i.e., downed deadwood of a minimum size) is used as the forest health variable of interest; however, the underlying concepts can be applied to analyses of other variables as well.

Keywords: Analysis, ancillary data, coarse woody debris, estimation, FIA, forest health data.

Acknowledgments

The authors thank Stan Zarnoch, Sarah Jovan, and one anonymous reviewer for their helpful suggestions and comments.

Introduction

The Forest Inventory and Analysis (FIA) program of the U.S. Forest Service is responsible for collecting forest inventory data on an annual basis. The inventory has two main field components: 1) a set of nationwide ground plots on which standard mensuration variables, such as tree species, heights, and diameters, are measured, and 2) a subset of plots where forest health variables, such as down woody material, lichens, soils, and understory vegetation, are also measured. The full set of plots is called phase 2 (P2) plots. The plots having forest health measurements are called phase 3 (P3) plots.

This design arose from the merger of two different inventory schemes: the FIA program, which traditionally measured the standard mensuration variables (e.g., P2 plots), and forest health monitoring (FHM), which measured the forest health attributes (e.g., P3 plots). Prior to the merger of the field measurement portions of the two programs, the plot designs were incompatible and were not necessarily colocated, or measured at the same time. When the two monitoring efforts merged, a common plot design was adopted, along with colocated plots, and same-time measurements of both sets of variables.

While some logistical efficiencies have been gained by jointly measuring the P2 variables and P3 variables on the P3 plots, relatively little statistical efficiency in terms of more precise estimates of P3 variables has yet been created by this merger. Part of this lack of increased statistical efficiency has been due to the nature of the two original programs. As an inventory program, FIA's main outputs are county and State totals of variables such as forest area and tree volume and changes in those totals. FHM primarily had a long-term monitoring approach, whose main goals were status, trends, and changes in forest health. While the FIA program continued to produce State totals using P2 plots, the FHM portion of the merged program has continued to use just the P3 plots. With the new emphasis on estimates of carbon stocks, there is an increased need to estimate State totals for some of the P3 variables, particularly down woody material and soils. While State totals can be calculated from the P3 plots, the precision of these estimates can be poor due to the lower P3 sampling intensity. The precision can be improved by incorporating auxiliary information such as information from the P2 variables.

The objective of this publication is to explore and suggest methods to analysts wanting to incorporate other auxiliary data into their analysis of the P3 data. While we do emphasize using the P2 data and estimating population totals, we realize that other sources of data and other objectives might interest analysts. We make some pre-analysis suggestions including ideas for checking for problem data. Because the goals, variables, and amount of available data differ for each project, there is no possible one-size-fits-all type of statistical analysis. Therefore, a general review of different statistical techniques that could be used is provided. This review is not meant to be exhaustive. Also, our goal is not to create a text book with instructions on how to run each type of analysis, but rather to give the readers a sufficient intuitive feel for each method to help them decide which statistical method will best fit their needs. Chapters 1 through 3 contain suggestions for preparing and exploring the data. Chapters 4 through 7 contain reviews of possible methods of analysis.

Example Dataset

To increase the cohesion between the different chapters, examples of the analyses discussed in each chapter used the same dataset. These data are from the State of Michigan and were obtained from the FIA program. Data are collected in three phases. Phase 1 is the development of a stratification scheme using remotely-sensed data. Under the current FIA sampling design where plot locations are fixed over time, stratification occurs after the plot locations are selected, thus the term post-stratification. Currently, the post-stratification for Michigan is based on canopy cover information obtained from the national land cover database 2001 map product (Homer and others 2004). Using plot location information, a percent cover was assigned to each plot. Plots were then aggregated into groups based on cover classes 0–5, 6–50, 51–65, 66–80, and 81–100 percent. Stratum weights were determined by dividing the number of map pixels in each stratum by the total number of map pixels in the population.

The second phase (P2) of data collection is measuring sample plots on the ground for the usual suite of variables such as tree species, diameter at breast height, and height, site index, forest type, stand age, etc. (U.S. Department of Agriculture Forest Service 2007). These data include 13,274 P2 plots measured between 2002–06, which comprises the entire sample in the State. A unique feature of the plot measurement protocols is the delineation of separate conditions (Scott and others 2005). This entails describing a boundary line between areas on the plot that differ in certain attributes.

P3 forest health indicator data is collected on a subset of the P2 plots. The down woody material indicator is one of the forest health indicators collected on the P3 plots. Specifically, measurements of coarse woody debris were used to calculate the amount of coarse woody debris carbon per acre in each plot condition (Woodall and Monleon 2008). The data were from 468 conditions on 381 P3 plots in Michigan measured between 2002–06.

Data Sources for Forest Health Data

Before starting any analysis of the forest health indicator variables, the analyst needs to have an understanding of the forest health indicator. Each indicator has a unique reference publication: crowns (Schomaker and others 2007), down woody material (Woodall and Monleon 2008), lichen (Will-Wolf 2010), ozone (Smith and others 2007; Smith and others 2008), soils (O'Neill and others 2005), and vegetation diversity and structure (Schulz and others 2009). The field manuals for both the forest indicators (P3) and the standard forest mensuration variables (P2) can be found at http://www.fia.fs.fed.us/library/field-guides-methods-proc/. The documentation for the database for both the forest indicators and the standard mensuration variables can be found at http://www.fia.fs.fed.us/library/database-documentation/.

The data can be accessed from the FIA DataMart at http://apps.fs.fed.us/fiadb-downloads/datamart.html. However, going through http://www.fia.fs.fed.us/tools-data/default.asp to get to the DataMart will make accessing customer support easier. Most of the forest indicator data tables include a variable named PLT_CN. This is the control number of the P2 plot measurement as it appears as CN in the PLOT table. Since the tables for the other standard mensuration variables, such as CONDITION and TREE, include the variable PLT_CN, this variable can be used to connect the forest health indicator data to the mensuration data. Due to the Food Security Act of 1985, FIA is not allowed to give out exact plot coordinates. Therefore, only approximate coordinates are given. If you need to have exact coordinates, you will need to contact FIA's Spatial Data Services at http://www.fia.fs.fed.us/tools-data/spatial/default.asp.

Literature Cited

Homer, C.; Huang, C.; Yang, L. [and others]. 2004. Development of a 2001 national landcover database for the United States. Photogrammetric Engineering Remote Sensing. 70(7): 829–840.

O'Neill, K.P.; Amacher, M.C.; Perry, C.H. 2005. Soils as an indicator of forest health: a guide to the collection, analysis, and interpretation of soil indicator data in the forest inventory and analysis program. Gen. Tech. Rep. NC–258. St. Paul, MN: U.S. Department of Agriculture Forest Service, North Central Research Station. 53 p.

Schomaker, M.E.; Zarnoch, S.J.; Bechtold, W.A. [and others]. 2007. Crown condition classification: a guide to data collection and analysis. Gen. Tech. Rep. SRS–102. Asheville, NC: U.S. Department of Agriculture Forest Service, Southern Research Station. 78 p.

Schulz, B.K.; Bechtold, W.A.; Zarnoch, S.J. 2009. Sampling and estimation procedures for the vegetation diversity and structure indicator. Gen. Tech. Rep. PNW–GTR–781. Portland, OR: U.S. Department of Agriculture Forest Service, Pacific Northwest Research Station. 53 p.

Scott, C.T.; Bechtold, W.A.; Reams, G.A. [and others]. 2005. Sample-based estimators used by the forest inventory and analysis national information management system. In: Bechtold, W.A.; Patterson, P.L., eds. The enhanced Forest Inventory and Analysis program—national sampling design and estimation procedures. Gen. Tech. Rep. SRS–80. Asheville, NC: U.S. Department of Agriculture Forest Service, Southern Research Station. 43–67.

Smith, G.C; Smith, W.D.; Coulston, J.W. 2007. Ozone bioindicator sampling and estimation. Gen. Tech. Rep. NRS–20. Newtown Square, PA: U.S. Department of Agriculture Forest Service, Northern Research Station. 100 p.

Smith, G.C.; Coulston, J.W.; O'Connell, B.M. 2008. Ozone bioindicators and forest health: a guide to the evaluation, analysis, and interpretation of the ozone injury data in the forest inventory and analysis program. Gen. Tech. Rep. NRS–34. Newtown Square, PA: U.S. Department of Agriculture Forest Service, Northern Research Station. 100 p.

U.S. Department of Agriculture Forest Service. 2007. Forest inventory and analysis National P2 field guide. Version 4.0. Arlington VA: U.S. Department of Agriculture Forest Service, Forest Inventory and Analysis. http://fia.fs.fed.us/library/field-guides-methods-proc/. [Date accessed: July, 2012].

Will-Wolf, S. 2010. Analyzing lichen indicator data in the forest inventory and analysis program. Gen. Tech. Rep. PNW–GTR–818. Portland, OR: U.S. Department of Agriculture Forest Service, Pacific Northwest Research Station. 62 p.

Woodall, C.; Monleon V.J. 2008. Sampling protocol, estimation procedures, and analytical guidelines for down woody materials indicator of the FIA program. Gen Tech. Rep. NRS–22 Newtown Square, PA: U.S. Department of Agriculture Forest Service, Northern Research Station. 68 p.

Section 1—Exploratory Analysis

Chapter 1: Reviewing Knowledge of the Biology

David Gartner, Christopher Woodall, and James Westfall

There are statistical procedures called data mining techniques, originally used primarily in marketing and credit analysis, that are designed to require very little prior knowledge about the relationships between the predicted variable (called the dependant variable or target variable) and the variables used to predict/model that variable (called the independent variables or the predictor variables). Some of these techniques are discussed in chapter 7. However, these techniques usually require very large datasets (>2,000 observations). Most analysis of phase 3 (P3) variables will not have the luxury of datasets this large. The analysis methods for smaller datasets usually require assumptions about the relationships between the target variable and the predictor variables. Therefore, taking time to consider what is known about the relationships between the target variable and the predictor variables will usually be helpful. Writing out the expected relationships helps clarify relationships and point to expected results.

Since we are using coarse woody debris carbon (CWD_c) as the target variable in our example analyses, we are including an analysis of the biological/physical relationships between coarse woody debris (CWD) and the phase 2 (P2) variables. This analysis is broken into two parts. The first section describes the expected relationships between CWD_c and the independent variables of interest. The second section looks at the independent variables of interest and attempts to deduce their expected effect on CWD_c.

Expected Relationships

The change in the amount of CWD_c will be the difference between CWD_c accretion and CWD_c losses (Woodall 2010). CWD_c accretion is the result of woody biomass mortality and subsequent downfall (Gough and others 2007), a forest ecosystem dynamic that is inherently linked to the ecology of CWD (Harmon and others 1986). As CWD is often not rooted to sites, it is often subjected to disturbance events such as removal by flooding. Under undisturbed conditions, most of the CWD_c losses are expected to occur due to normal decomposition processes. Other sources of CWD_c losses are fire and human intervention (e.g., harvesting and site preparation).

Because the main source of CWD accretion will be branch loss and tree mortality, CWD inputs are expected to be their lowest at stand initiation with subsequent increase as stands age. Aside from CWD inputs, there can be tremendous residual CWD at stand initiation due to prior disturbance

events (e.g., wildfire or harvest). Therefore, in the absence of major disturbances, CWD_c stocks may be related to stand age, stand density, stand volume, growth rate, and possibly tree species composition (Janisch and Harmon 2002, Woodall and Westfall 2009). Since tree mortality will involve the loss of the remaining branches (Domke and others 2011), there may be a correlation between CWD_c and the volume of standing dead trees. Stochastic disturbance events can create exceptions to this general trend (Woodall and Nagel 2007, Woodall and Westfall 2009).

Decomposition can be broadly ascribed to a complex of abiotic and biotic processes entwined with the attributes of each downed deadwood piece itself (Harmon and others 1986, Yin 1999). Although fungi and microinvertebrates may be a primary driver of wood decay (Käärik 1974), certain environmental factors such as moisture/oxygen availability and wood attributes such as lignin content affect wood decay rates to an unknown extent (Harmon and others 2000, Freschet and others 2012). Hence, the variables in the Forest Inventory and Analysis database that may be useful for modeling CWD decay rates are those related to climate (e.g., physiographic class or latitude) and individual species attributes (e.g., CWD species) (Yin 1999).

Flooding can either deposit or remove CWD. While intense fires will consume CWD_c, fires can kill standing trees, creating an influx of CWD_c at a later date (Kashian and others 2006). In addition to wildfires, varying utilization rates at harvest sites will in turn result in varying resultant CWD_c stocks (Radtke and others 2004). However, if intense harvesting methods like chip milling are used, the remaining amount of CWD_c may be small. In the P2 database, wildfires are classified as a disturbance and harvesting is classified as a treatment, as is prescribed burning.

Expected Effects

Stand age is expected to be among the most important variables in the prediction of CWD_c, with the amount expected to increase with stand age (Radtke and others 2004). Increased stand density in terms of either basal area and/or stocking is expected to create increased inputs to CWD_c, but minimally affect the decomposition rate. Therefore, basal area is expected to be positively correlated with CWD_c. Site index is the expected height of the stand at a given 'base' age. The larger the site index, the faster the stand is expected to grow. Faster tree growth is an indicator of more rapid stand development with resultant increased rates of branch loss and tree mortality due to self-thinning (Oliver and Larson 1996). Therefore, site index is expected to be positively correlated to CWD_c.

Species composition, as denoted by forest type, might affect both the amount of CWD due to differences in branching patterns and the effects of different lignin contents on decomposition rates (Harmon and others 1986). Dry physiographic classes are expected to have more CWD_c than mesic physiographic classes with the same site index (Woodall and Liknes 2008). Hydric physiographic classes are also expected to have more CWD_c than mesic physiographic classes with the same site index, with the caveat that stands on riverine floodplains are expected to be highly variable (Woodall and others 2012). Since both dry and hydric physiographic classes usually have lower site indices than mesic physiographic classes, care will need to be taken to remember this relationship when investigating the effect of physiographic class on CWD_c stocks.

The objective of this initial analytical step is to create a short list of variables for further data exploration. There is a tenuous balance between including too few predictor variables in the data exploration that results in correspondingly weak models, and including too many predictor variables which increases the probability that the data exploration process will identify spurious relationships between predictor and target variables (Woodall and Westfall 2012). Although, there is no strict rule for determining which variables to include in the data exploration, suggestions from ecological literature can often provide direction. From our process of describing the biological effects of P2 variables on the volume of CWD, we have decided to include the following variables in our analyses: stand age, basal area per condition acre, forest type, site index, disturbances, harvesting, fire, site preparation, volume of dead trees, physiographic class, and decomposition season length.

Literature Cited

Domke, G.M.; Woodall, C.W.; Smith, J.E. 2011. Accounting for density reduction and structural loss in standing dead trees: implications for forest biomass and carbon stock estimates in the United States. Carbon Balance and Management. 6: 14.

Freschet, G.T.; Weedon, J.T.; Aerts, R. [and others]. 2012. Interspecific differences in wood decay rates: insights from a new short-term method to study long-term wood decomposition. Journal of Ecology. 100: 161–170.

Gough, C.M.; Vogel, C.S.; Kazanski, C. [and others]. 2007. Coarse woody debris and the carbon balance of a north temperate forest. Forest Ecology and Management. 244: 60–67.

Harmon, M.E.; Franklin, J.F.; Swanson, F.J. [and others]. 1986. Ecology of coarse woody debris in temperate ecosystems. Advances in Ecological Research. 15: 133–302.

Harmon, M.E.; Krankina, O.N.; Sexton, J. 2000. Decomposition vectors: a new approach to estimating woody detritus decomposition dynamics. Canadian Journal of Forest Research. 30: 76–84.

Janisch, J.E.; Harmon, M.E. 2002. Successional changes in live and dead wood carbon stores: implications for net ecosystem productivity. Tree Physiology. 22: 77–89.

Käärik, A.A. 1974. Decomposition of wood. In: Dickenson, C.H.; Pugh, G.J.F., eds. Biology of plant litter decomposition. London: Academic Press: 129–174.

Kashian, D.M.; Romme, W.H.; Tinker, D.B.; [and others]. 2006. Carbon storage on landscapes with stand-replacing fires. BioScience. 56: 598–606.

Oliver, C.D.; Larson, B.C., 1996. Forest stand dynamics. Updated edition. New York: John Wiley. 521 p.

Radtke, P.J.; Prisley, S.P.; Amateis, R.L. [and others]. 2004. A proposed model for deadwood C production and decay in loblolly pine plantations. Environmental Management. 33, Supplement 1: S56–S64

Woodall, C.W. 2010. Carbon flux of down woody materials in forests of North Central United States. International Journal of Forest Research. 2010: 1–9.

Woodall, C.W.; Liknes, G.C. 2008. Climatic regions as an indicator of forest coarse and fine woody debris carbon stocks in the United States. Carbon Balance and Management. 3: 5.

Woodall, C.W.; Nagel, L.M. 2007. Down woody fuel loadings dynamics of a large-scale blowdown in northern Minnesota. Forest Ecology and Management. 247: 194–199.

Woodall, C.W.; Walters, B.F.; Westfall, J.A. 2012. Tracking downed dead wood in forests over time: Development of a piece matching algorithm for line intercept sampling. Forest Ecology and Management. 277: 196–204.

Woodall, C.W.; Westfall, J.A. 2012. Curious or spurious correlations within a large-scale forest inventory. In: McWilliams, W.; Roesch, F.A., eds. Monitoring across borders: 2010 joint meeting of the forest inventory and analysis (FIA) symposium and the southern mensurationists. e-Gen. Tech. Rep. SRS–157. Asheville, NC: U.S. Department of Agriculture Forest Service, Southern Research Station: 39–43.

Woodall, C.W.; Westfall, J.A. 2009. Relationships between the stocking levels of live trees and dead tree attributes in forests of the United States. Forest Ecology and Management. 258: 2602–2608.

Yin, X. 1999. The decay of forest woody debris: numerical modeling and implications based on some 300 data cases from North America. Oecologia. 121(1): 81–98.

Chapter 2: Data Screening

David Gartner, James Westfall, and Christopher Woodall

"A statistical analysis is only as good as the data being analyzed. . . . It has been said that one should never trust a large dataset to be correct. Errors are unavoidable and steps must be taken to deal with them. A few unfortunate errors may cause a statistical analysis to be worthless or, even worse, misleading." (Johnson 1998)

Almost all large datasets will have either data errors or highly unusual observations (outliers). People will occasionally make measurement errors and typos, and electronic recording devices will go out of calibration. Occasionally, stochastic disturbances can greatly affect the data, such as the July 4, 1999 downburst that flattened trees in large areas of the Boundary Water Canoe Area (bwcawiki.org 2009). Both errors and highly unusual observations can cause problems for statistical analysis. Therefore, as a general rule, you should check your data for these potential problems.

Understanding the data entry process will help recognize types and sources of data entry errors. The first step to understanding the data entry process is understanding what variables are being entered, and how each variable is used. Coarse woody debris carbon (CWD_c) is recorded in one of two ways: either as single pieces of coarse woody debris (CWD), or as CWD piles. No CWD piles were recorded in our example dataset. The single pieces of CWD are sampled using a line transect method. Three transects radiating from the center of each subplot are used to sample CWD. Each piece of CWD that crosses one of the transects has the following measurements recorded: small end diameter (down to 3 inches), diameter where the CWD intersects the transect, the large end diameter, the length between the small end diameter and the large end diameter, and the location on the transect. The volume and mass of each piece is calculated from the small end diameter, the large end diameter, and the length. Therefore, the variables whose data entry errors that are most likely to cause spurious CWD_c values are the small end diameter, the large end diameter, and the length.

The data entry program used in our example CWD_c dataset is called Mobile Integrated Data Acquisition System (MIDAS). MIDAS requires that all of the relevant variables have been entered before the observation is transmitted. For example, if the field crew enters a tree with a diameter, MIDAS will require that a height and a species code, etc., are also entered. Therefore, MIDAS will make sure that all CWD pieces have a small end diameter, a large end diameter, and a length. For a complete description of these variables see the Down Woody Materials (DWM) Field Manual 4.0 at http://www.fia.fs.fed.us/library/field-guides-methods-proc/. MIDAS will also make sure that the data entered are within the acceptable range for each variable. However, MIDAS does not check for the relationships

between two variables. For example, MIDAS will not check for problems in the relationship between tree heights and tree diameters. Therefore, we will concern ourselves with measurement errors and typos, and unusual observations. Because the data is entered for each piece of CWD which is used to calculate a volume and then summed by condition, the measurement errors and typos will be found by looking at the CWD piece data and the unusual observation will be found by looking at the condition totals. We will start with the CWD piece data.

Checking for Measurement Errors and Typos

The easiest method for detecting potential problem observations are graphs. There are also statistical tests to detect potential problem observations. While these methods detect possible errors, they will, at best, produce probabilities that the observation is an error. Proving that an observation is an error is very difficult. Usually, either a probability threshold is used or a subjective decision is made for each observation.

For continuous variables, scatter plots of two variables are a good place to start. We have included graphs of small-end diameter versus large-end diameter (fig. 2.1), length versus large-end diameter (fig. 2.2), and length versus small-end diameter (fig. 2.3). The scatter plot of large-end diameter versus small-end diameter (fig. 2.1), in addition to showing two extreme points (one with a large-end diameter >30 inches, and the other with a small-end diameter of 21 inches), shows several observations with large-end diameters that are larger than most of the rest of the observations with the same small-end diameters. However, those observations do not fall as far out of the range of the rest of the data as some of the lengths found in the scatter plots of large-end diameter versus length (fig. 2.2) and small-end diameter versus length (fig. 2.3) which show a group of observations with very large lengths.

Two dimensional graphs limit your view to two variables at a time. Alternatives that allow for more information per graph include 3-D graphs, and methods that graph each observation such as star graphs and Chernoff face graphs (Chernoff 1973). Since Chernoff face graphs and star graphs create a graph for each observation, they are not practicable for large datasets.

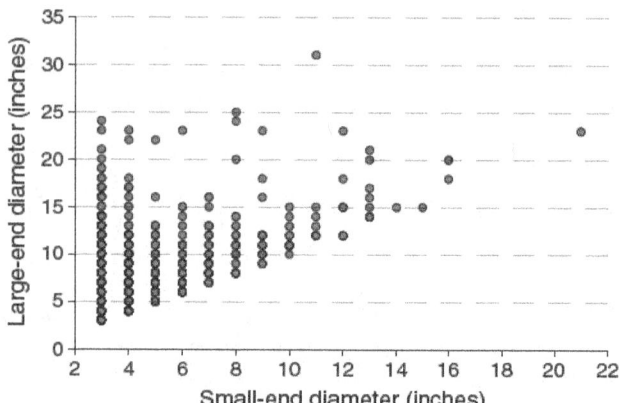

Figure 2.1—Large-end diameter versus small-end diameter.

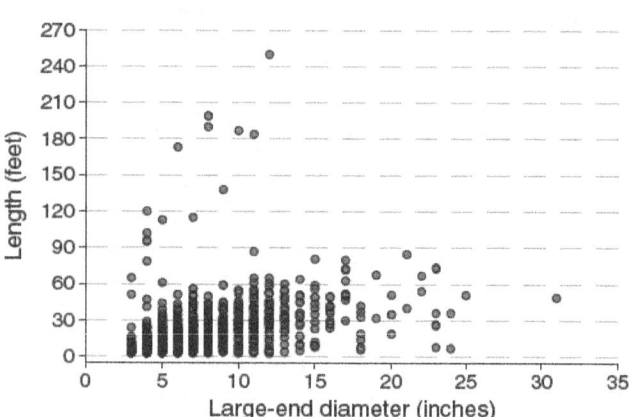

Figure 2.2—Length versus large-end diameter.

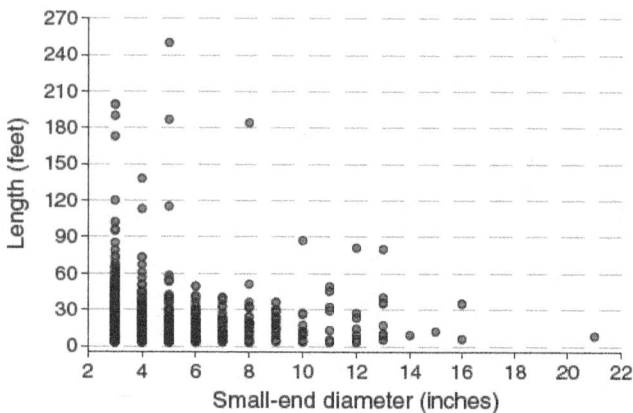

Figure 2.3—Length versus small-end diameter.

Since the CWD diameters are measured in inches and the CWD length is measured in feet, several observations can fall on the same graph symbol on the scatter graphs. To help differentiate between the graph symbols with multiple observations and those with only one observation, we created a box graph (Tukey 1977) of length by large-end diameter (fig. 2.4). The line in the middle of the box is the median. The top of the box is the 75th percentile. The bottom of the box is the 25th percentile. The whiskers extend out from the box to the last observation that is <1.5 times the interquartile range from the end of the box. The circles represent observations outside this range, that need to be considered as potential errors or unusual observations.

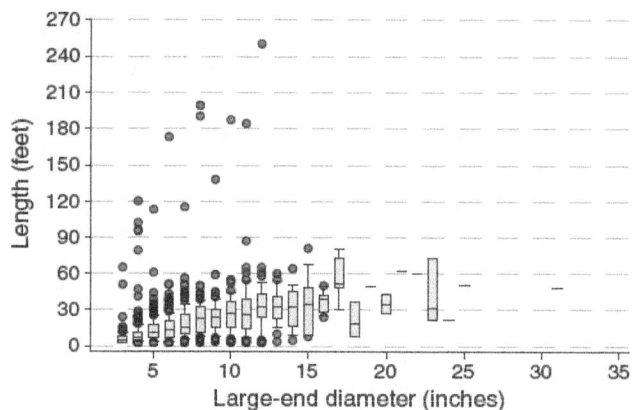

Figure 2.4—Initial box plot of length by large-end diameter.

Dealing With Potential Measurement Errors and Typos

Once an observation is determined to be a problem, there are five main possible actions: 1) leave the observation in the dataset unchanged, 2) remove the observation from the dataset, 3) replacing the erroneous value with what you think is the proper value based on the erroneous value (data editing), 4) replace the erroneous value with what you think is the proper value based on the values of the other variables (single imputation), and 5) replace the erroneous value with several different potentially proper values, rerunning the analysis with each different potentially proper values using a method called multiple imputation (Rubin 1987).

Your options for dealing with problem observations are affected by how sure you are of your ability to determine the correct values. If you are not sure that the value is an error, leave it in the dataset. If you have few errors and very little information as to what the correct value is, consider deleting the observations. If there exists a procedural problem that causes some observations to have errors in a systematic manner, use the data editing approach. If one of the values in the observation appears to be an error, but the other values are not, you might want to use one of the imputation methods. Examples of this type case appear in figure 2.4, where the values for large end diameter look reasonable, but the values for some of the length values do not look reasonable. Imputation would be choosing a reasonable length value based on the length values for other observations of the same large end diameter. Single imputation consists of choosing one reasonable length value, while multiple imputation consists of choosing several reasonable length values based on the large end diameter value. The more observations with erroneous values and the greater the variation in the reasonable replacement values, the greater the need to use multiple imputation. Unfortunately, multiple imputation procedures are complex and a good knowledge of multiple imputation is needed before using them.

In the case of CWD, removing an observed piece of CWD from the dataset due to an erroneous length value affects the condition level summed CWD volume. Therefore, if we deleted individual CWD piece observations, we would affect the condition level values. So, we wanted to avoid deleting CWD piece observations. There is a CWD protocol that occasionally causes systematic errors. For CWD, lengths are measured in integer feet. For the mensuration data, lengths are measured in tenths of feet. The portable data recorder's mensuration data entry screen does not show the decimal point. Therefore, while the mensuration data entry screen interprets a tree height value of "100" as 10 feet, the CWD data entry screen interprets a CWD length value of "100" as 100 feet. The cruisers are required to remember which data measurement uses which data format. If the cruiser uses the phase 2 data format for entering the DWM data, then their recorded lengths should be 10 times the correct length. We decided to assume that the large observed lengths were probably due to this error. Therefore, we adjusted these lengths by dividing them by 10 and then rounding to the nearest integer. After adjusting the largest lengths, the new box plots (fig. 2.5) looks much more reasonable. There are still a few observations that look questionable, and could also be adjusted. However, the actual cutoff point between lengths that are adjusted and those which are not adjusted is subjective.

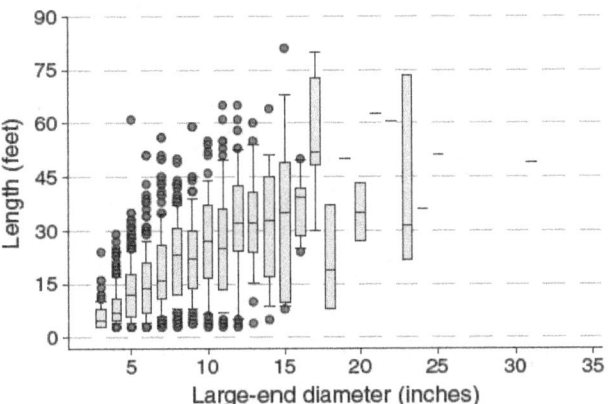

Figure 2.5—Box plot of lengths by large-end diameter after data editing.

We also looked into the observation with the largest large end diameter (31 inches). While this diameter was larger than any of the diameter at breast height (d.b.h.) of any of the living trees, it was close to the size of the largest trees. Since we were not sure that this measurement was actually an error, we left the observation unchanged in the dataset.

Checking for Condition Level Outliers

If the forest health indicator has individual observations that are used to calculate a plot or condition level value, then the condition level values should be checked for unusual observations. For CWD, this would mean checking for conditions with very large CWD volume values that might have been caused by a rare disturbance like a major windstorm. The methods for checking unusual condition level values are the same as checking for unusual measurements.

The options for dealing with the unusual condition level values are limited. Since the measurement errors and typos have been removed, the data editing option doesn't truly exist. If the unusual values are sufficiently rare, then very little will be gained by using the imputation methods. The main options are leaving the value in and deleting the observation. The main consideration in this decision is whether or not the cause of the unusual value is to be considered as part of the population. For instance, if you are working with crowns and a few plots have experienced a crown fire, you might want to get the Forest Service maps of crown fire areas and treat them as different population than the areas without crown fires. In this case, you would separate the plots that have experienced crown fires from the main dataset.

To determine if there were any unusual condition level observations in the CWD dataset, we generated a histogram of the amounts of CWD_c (fig. 2.6). At the larger amounts of CWD, the number of plots gets very sparse. However, there do not appear to be any observations that appear to have been caused by catastrophic disturbances. So, we decided to not delete any of the condition level observations. Now that we have a cleaned dataset, we can feel more confident about any analysis we perform.

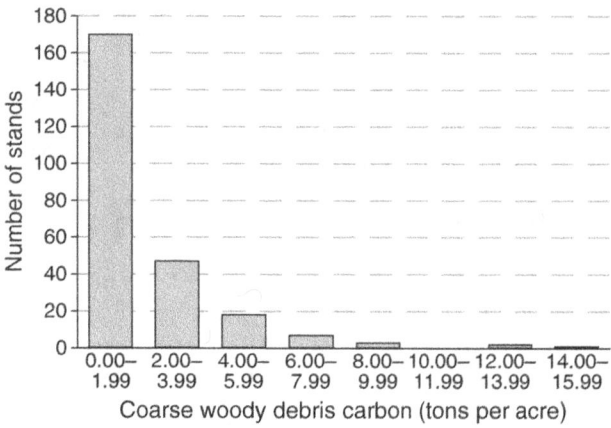

Figure 2.6—Histogram of conditions grouped by down woody carbon.

Literature Cited

Bwcawiki.org. 2009. Fourth of July Blowdown. http://www.bwcawiki.org/wiki/Fourth_of_July_Blowdown . [Date accessed: January 20, 2012].

Chernoff, H. 1973. The use of faces to represent points in K-dimensional space graphically, Journal of the American Statistical Association. 68(342): 361–368.

Johnson, D.E. 1998. Applied multivariate methods for data analysts. Pacific Grove, CA: Brooks/Cole Publishing Company. 563 p.

Rubin, D.B. 1987. Multiple imputation for nonresponse in surveys. New York: John Wiley. 320 p.

Tukey, J.W. 1977. Exploratory data analysis. Reading, MA: Addison-Wesley. 688 p.

U.S. Department of Agriculture Forest Service. 2005. http://www.fia.fs.fed.us/library/field-guides-methods-proc/.

Chapter 3: Data Exploration

David Gartner

Now that the example dataset has been screened, the possible relationships suggested in the analysis in chapter 1 can be tested against the data. If both the predictor and target variables are continuous, then scatter graphs will show the relationship better than correlations because correlations are restricted to linear relationships. For very large datasets, there may be so many observations that the symbols blend together and hide the differences in densities within the graph. This is not likely to happen with forest health indicator data. For continuous target variables and categorical predictor variables, box and whisker graphs work well.

Univariate Relationships

Only three stands recorded fire as a disturbance, which is not enough to test for the effects of fire. The scatter graph of coarse woody debris carbon (CWD_c) versus age (fig. 3.1) shows three observations with unusually high levels of carbon. For plots >30 years old, there is a weak general tendency for older plots to have more carbon. For plots <30 years old, there is a tendency for older plots to have less carbon. This corresponds well to the assumption in chapter 1 that, while a new stand may have varying amounts of CWD_c leftover from the previous stand, this initial amount of CWD_c will decompose over time. Harvested stands had more CWD_c than unharvested stands (fig. 3.2). An analysis of variance (ANOVA) showed that the difference between harvested stands and unharvested stands was statistically significant. The volume of live trees (fig. 3.3) does not show a relationship with CWD_c, while the volume of dead trees does (fig. 3.4). Since there are several physiographic classes with only one stand, the classes were collapsed to the main soil moisture classes of xeric, mesic, and hydric. While an ANOVA showed a significant affect of soil moisture class on CWD_c, the xeric mean was significantly different from the mesic mean, but neither the xeric nor the mesic mean were significantly different from the hydric mean (fig. 3.5). The graph of CWD_c versus latitude (fig. 3.6) suggests an increase in latitude is related to an increase in CWD_c. Since an increase in latitude corresponds with a decrease in the decomposition season, this observed relationship conforms to biological theory. There is no apparent relationship between CWD_c and either site index or elevation.

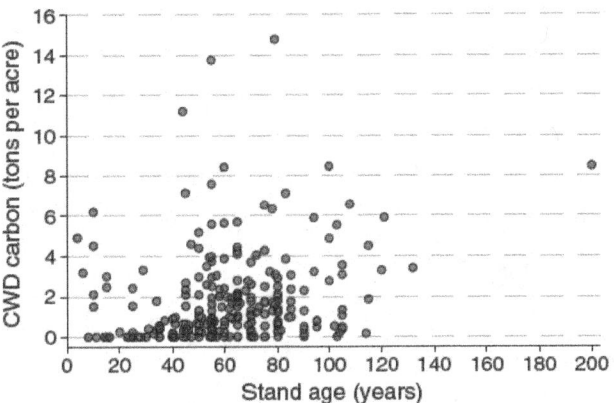

Figure 3.1—Coarse woody debris (CWD) carbon versus stand age.

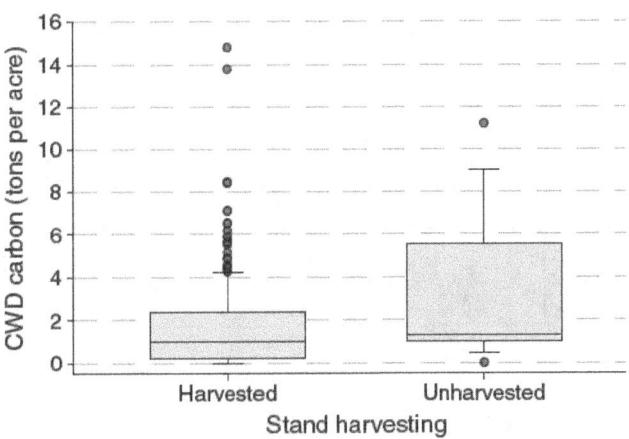

Figure 3.2—Coarse woody debris (CWD) carbon by stand harvesting.

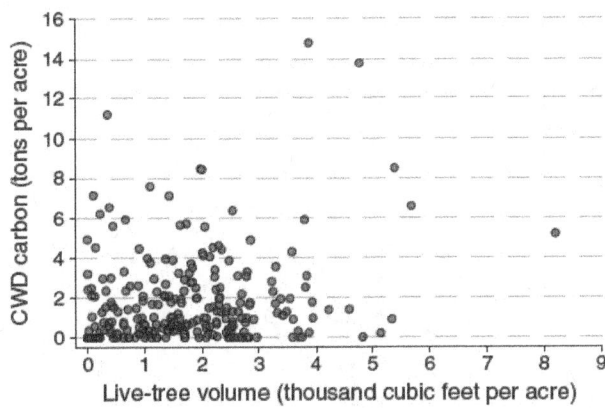

Figure 3.3—Coarse woody debris (CWD) carbon versus live-tree volume.

11

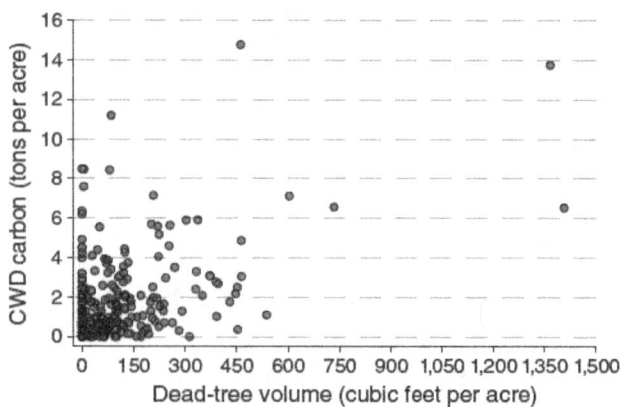

Figure 3.4—Coarse woody debris (CWD) carbon versus dead-tree volume.

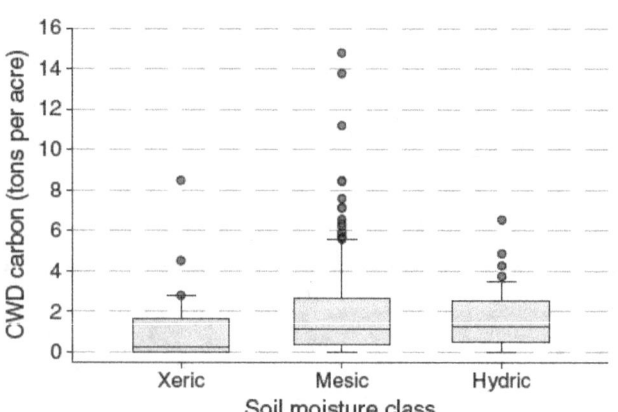

Figure 3.5—Coarse woody debris (CWD) carbon by soil moisture class.

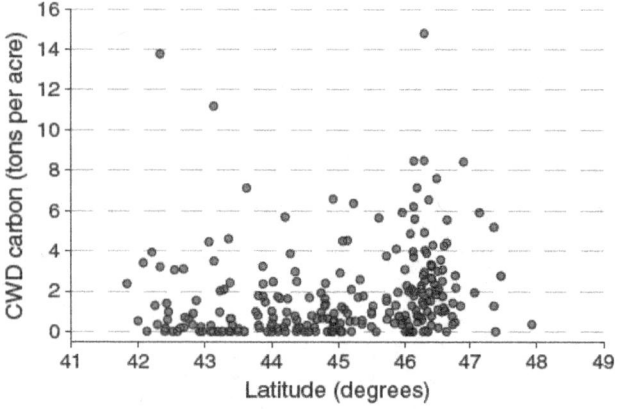

Figure 3.6—Coarse woody debris (CWD) carbon versus latitude.

Multivariate Linear Data Exploration

Looking for the relationship of several predictor variables and the target variables can be difficult to do graphically. One method for looking at relationships between the target variable and several predictor variables is linear regression. While linear regression is designed for target variables that are normally distributed, the lack of normality will cause the parameter estimates to have larger variances and cause the distribution for testing the parameters to change. Since the current goal is to determine if the data conforms to our analyses of the literature from chapter 1, as opposed to formal model development, we are not going to concern ourselves with the lack of normality.

Since the relationship between CWD_c and the stand characteristics in harvested stands is expected to be different from unharvested stands, we put the harvested stands into a separate group. Since the CWD_c in young stands is assumed to have originated with the previous stand, we separated them from the older stands that generate their own CWD_c inputs. There are 15 stands in the harvested stand group, 29 stands in the young unharvested stand group, and 204 stands in the older unharvested stand group. Each group was analyzed using SAS's (SAS Institute Inc. 2003) PROC REG using the stepwise model selection procedure. The stepwise model selection procedure finds the best predictor variable and adds it to the model if the predictor variable's parameter is significantly different from zero. If, as new predictor variables are included, one of the predictor variables' parameter becomes nonsignificant, that predictor variable is dropped from the model. We used 0.05 for the required significance level when interpreting the results. The predictor variables used in the analysis are age, volume of dead trees, volume of live trees, latitude, a variable indicating mesic sites, and an indicator variable for hydric sites.

Results of Stepwise Regression

No predictor variables were selected during the SAS stepwise regression for the amount of CWD_c in harvested stands. The theoretical model for young unharvested stands is that the CWD_c pieces are remnants from the previous stand that decay with time. The only predictor variable with a significant parameter is age (table 3.1). Since the parameter is negative, the data supports the theoretical model. The first predictor variable to enter the linear model of CWD_c for older unharvested stands is the volume of dead trees, followed by age, and followed by the indicator variable for mesic soil conditions (table 3.2). All three parameters are

Table 3.1—Linear regression results for young stands

Variable	Parameter estimate	p-value
Intercept	3.06032	0.0009
Stand age	-0.10285	0.0187
MSE	2.4911	

MSE = mean squared error.

Table 3.2—Linear regression results for older stands

Variable	Parameter estimate	p-value
Intercept	-1.08049	0.0144
Dead volume	0.00589	0.0001
Stand age	0.02508	0.0001
Soil2 (mesic)	0.64569	0.0146
MSE	3.13827	

MSE = mean squared error.

positive. The positive parameter for mesic sites suggests that the mesic sites are expected to have more CWD_c than xeric or hydric sites. However, we were not able to separate the effects of soil moisture from the effects of site index, so the increased amount of CWD on the mesic sites might be due to increased site quality on mesic sites.

Using Random Forest for Data Exploration

Random Forest (Breiman 2001) is a relatively new method for data exploration. Random Forest combines Classification And Regression Trees (CART) (Breiman and others 1984) with resampling methods. The CART process creates partitions in the axis of the predictor variables that split the target variables into similar groups. By creating enough partitions the CART process can handle nonlinear responses to the predictor variable. Random Forest takes a subsample of the data and of the parameter list and runs a CART. This process is repeated a large number of times with a different subsample each time. At the end of each tree, Random Forest predicts the value of the target variable for each observation not included in the subset. Random Forest has two different types of outputs. The Random Forest outputs with which people are most familiar are predicted values.

When making final predictions for an observation, Random Forest averages the predictions for each observation from the trees which did not include that observation in the subset. However, Random Forest also outputs a predictor variable importance metric. This metric is a comparison between the mean square error for the individual tree's predictions for the observations not used for trees with the variable and the same for trees without the variable. The actual variable is the difference between the two mean square errors as a percent of the mean square error from the trees that included the variable.

The predictor variable with the greatest effect on predicting CWD_c is dead-tree volume, followed by latitude, harvesting, stand age, live-tree volume, and soil moisture indicators (table 3.3). The only predictor variable to appear on this list that did not appear in the linear regression section is latitude. This suggests that the affect of latitude may not be linear.

Table 3.3—Random Forest variable importance results

Predictor variable	Percent increase in mean square error
Dead-tree volume	21.1
Latitude	12.7
Harvesting	8.9
Stand age	5.7
Live-tree volume	4.9
Mesic soil indicator	3.6
Hydric soil indicator	1.1

Ordination

Some target variables, such as species distributions, are not expected to be linearly related to the predictor variables. For target variables that are expected to have a symmetric unimodal response to the predictor variables, consider using canonical correspondence analysis (CCA) (ter Braak 1986). CCA is a descendant of correspondence analysis. Correspondence analysis (Hill 1974) originated from the analysis of tabular data that consisted of counts of different target variables, such as number of trees of each species, by site. The objective is to order both the sites and the species by giving them "scores" such that the highest counts for each species will occur on sites that have a score similar to their own (Hill 1974). Each additional set of scores are designed to be perpendicular to the original set of scores. While correspondence analysis does not require that the target variable be a symmetric unimodal response to the predictor variables (Greenacre 1984), ter Braak (1985) showed that assuming a symmetric unimodal response gives rise to correspondence analysis. ter Braak (1986) created CCA by regressing the site scores on a separate dataset of environmental variables gathered at each site. This allowed the species scores to be directly related to the environmental variables.

Correspondence analysis is designed for datasets with multiple target variables. Therefore, we included understory aboveground carbon, litter carbon, and duff carbon into the analysis of CWD_c. The independent variables used in the analysis are age, harvesting, volume of dead trees, volume of live trees, latitude, and indicator variables for xeric, mesic, and hydric soil moisture regimes. We realize that expecting the carbon variables to have smooth, unimodal, bell-shaped response to the stand variables is unrealistic. However, the main intent of this section is to demonstrate an ordination, rather than choosing ordination as a method to analyze the CWD_c data. Because correspondence analysis and CCA can create nonlinear effects in the axes, called the arch effect (Gauch and others 1977), we used detrending by segments (Hill and Gauch 1980; ter Braak 1986) in a variant called detrended canonical correspondence analysis or DCCA. CANOCO (ter Braak and Smilauer 2002) was used to run the analysis.

Results

The scores for the carbon pools (table 3.4) show that the scores for the understory carbon pool and the litter pool are very similar, which means that sites with large amounts of understory carbon are likely to have large amounts of litter carbon. The scores for CWD_c and duff carbon are both in different directions. The scores for the environmental variables in table 3.5 are graphed together with the carbon pool scores in a type of graph called a biplot (fig. 3.7). Because some of the environmental variable scores are so close together, the variables in table 3.5 are ordered by their score's position in the biplot clockwise starting with directly above. The biplot shows that xeric soil site score stands apart from the environmental variable scores in the direction of both understory aboveground carbon and litter carbon. The mesic soil site score is about midway between litter carbon and CWD_c. There are two clusters of environmental variable scores that point in the general direction

Table 3.4—DCCA scores for carbon pools

Variable name	Variable definition	Axis 1	Axis 2
CWD	Coarse woody debris carbon	1.4221	-0.1474
Understory	Aboveground understory carbon	1.1949	1.5806
Litter	Litter carbon	1.3096	1.7653
Duff	Duff carbon	-0.0039	0.8795

Table 3.5—DCCA scores for environmental variables

Variable name	Variable definition	Axis 1	Axis 2
xeric	Xeric soil condition	0.3017	0.1962
mesic	Mesic soil condition	0.56220	-0.0372
livevol	Volume of live trees	0.1956	-0.0833
harvest	Presence of harvesting	0.2207	-0.1175
latitud	Latitude	0.1710	-0.1502
deadvol	Volume of dead trees	0.0964	-0.3114
age	Stand age	0.0353	-0.1482
hydric	Hydric soil conditions	-0.6952	-0.0528

of the CWD_c score: live-tree volume, harvesting, latitude, dead-tree volume, and stand age. These two clusters along with mesic soil conditions are the environmental variable scores that are closest to the direction of CWD_c, which corresponds well with the Random Forest results. The closest relationship between the carbon pool scores and the environmental variable scores are hydric soils and duff carbon. This means that the highest levels of duff carbon are expected to be found on hydric soils.

While many versions of detrended correspondence analysis and CCA exist, currently the detrended CCA algorithm is proprietary to CANOCO (ter Braak and Smilauer 2002). Therefore, whether or not researchers use detrending may depend on whether or not they have the CANOCO software.

Conclusion

This step is not designed to be the end point of the analysis process, but rather the intent of the data exploration step is to take the variables from the theoretical analysis from chapter 1 and determine which variables warrant being used in a more formal analysis.

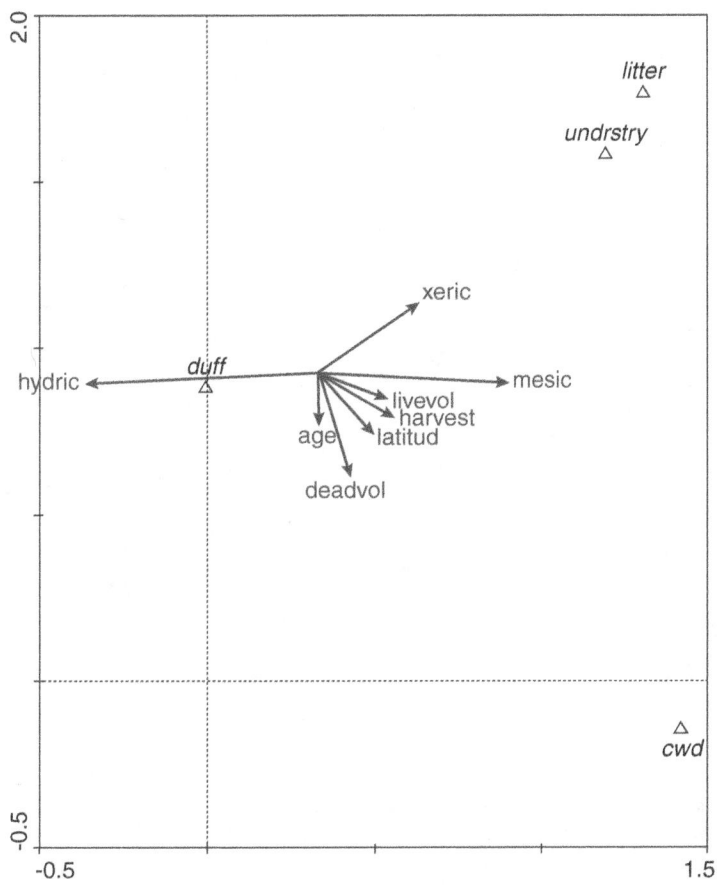

Figure 3.7—Biplot of results of DCCA of carbon pools on stand variables.

Literature Cited

Breiman, L. 2001. Random forests. Machine Learning. 45: 5–32.

Breiman, L.; Friedman, J.H.; Olshen, R.A.; Stone, C.J. 1984 Classification and regression trees. Boca Raton, FL: CRC Press. 368 p.

Gauch, H.G., Jr.; Whittaker, R.H.; Wentworth, T.R. 1977. A comparative study of reciprocal averaging and other ordination techniques. Journal of Ecology. 65: 157–174.

Greenacre, M.J. 1984. Theory and applications of correspondence analysis. London: Academic Press. 364 p.

Hill, M.O. 1974. Correspondence analysis: a neglected multivariate method. Applied Statistics. 23: 340–354.

Hill, M.O.; Gauch, H.G., Jr. 1980. Detrended correspondence analysis: an improved ordination technique. Vegetation. 42: 47–58.

SAS Institute, Inc. 2003 SAS/STAT user's guide, Version 9.1. Cary, NC: SAS Institite, Inc. [Pages unkown].

ter Braak, C.T.F. 1985. Correspondence analysis of incidence and abundance data: properties in terms of a unimodal response model. Biometrics. 41: 859–873.

ter Braak, C.T.F. 1986. Canonical correspondence analysis: a new eigenvector method for multivariate direct gradient analysis. Ecology. 67: 1167–1179.

ter Braak, C.T.F; Smilauer, P. 2002. CANOCO 4.5 Reference manual and canodraw for windows user's guide: software for canonical community ordination. Version 4.5. Ithaca, NY: Microcomputer Power. 500 p.

Section 2—Estimation

Chapter 4: Condition Level Estimates

David Gartner

The Forest Inventory and Analysis (FIA) mapped plot design can create problems not normally encountered in plot designs that limit the plot to a single stand. Two problems can occur because of the mapped plot design: some biological effects of mapped plots might affect your analysis, and the values from different stands on the same plot can be correlated. In addition, the values for your predictor variables on the phase 2 (P2) plots may be different from the range of values found on the phase 3 (P3) plots. These problems are easily overlooked and can cause unexpected consequences. If these problems can be resolved, then stand level estimates can be used in estimates of population totals, otherwise plot-level values may need to be used.

Theoretical Considerations

Possible Causes of Within-Plot Correlations

Most biological field plots are designed to be completely within a single stand. However, FIA plots are designed to allow multiple stands on a plot which can create complications. Some variables will be related to condition proportion such as the number of understory species. The number of species found in a sample area will increase with the size of the sample area, but the number of species per area will be highest for small plots and decrease as sample area increases (Barbour and others 1987). Therefore the number of species per unit area will depend in part on the size of the sample unit. When working with stand-level data, the sample area for that stand is the plot area within the stand, which can be calculated as the plot area times the condition proportion. Therefore, the condition proportion will affect the expected number of species found within a stand. Some variables will be affected by forest/nonforest boundaries. For example, a forest stand adjacent to a human-induced nonforest condition such as an agricultural field will get extra light in the understory which will affect the amount of understory cover and probably the species count and composition. The relationships between different stands on the same plot may also be affected by the form of the boundary. While some stands gradually merge from one forest type into another along an ecological gradient, other stands have distinct boundaries created either by water or by human intervention. How these differences affect an analysis will depend on the target variables and the predictor variables involved.

Data Ranges

The standard double sampling methods assume that the subsample (P3 plots) is a random sample of the original sample units (P2 plots). This leads to an assumption that the range of the P2 predictor variables (age, longitude, and volume of dead trees) on the P3 plots is about the same as on the P2 plots, and therefore the relationship between the P2 predictor variables and coarse woody debris carbon (CWD_c) on the P2 plots is the same as on the P3 plots. In order to test this assumption, we created side-by-side box plots of each of the P2 variables used in the linear regression model. While the ranges for stand age and plot latitude on the P2 plots are similar to the ranges for the P3 plots (figs. 4.1 and 4.2, respectively), the ranges for the volume of live trees per acre and the volume of dead trees per acre for the P2 stands are clearly different than the ranges for the P3 plots (figs. 4.3 and 4.4). Taking a subsample of a variable with a long-tailed distribution, such as live-tree volume per acre and dead-tree volume per acre, will usually cause the range to decrease. The decreased ranges found on the P3 plots do not necessarily indicate that the P3 plots are not a random subsample of P2 plots. The effect of this difference in ranges of predictor variables depends on whether the approximation to the relationship between the predictor variables and the target variables found within the range found on the P3 plots holds throughout the range found on P2 plots.

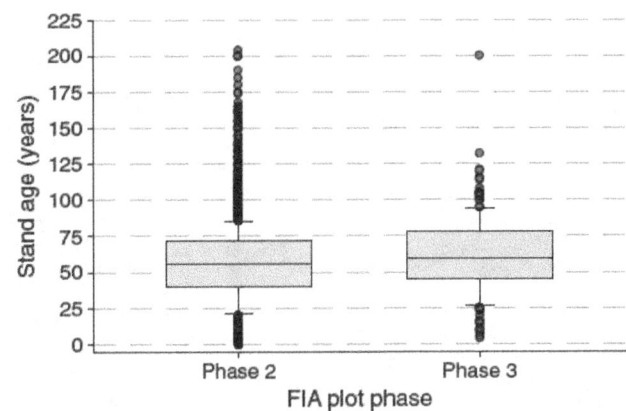

Figure 4.1—Stand ages for phase 2 and phase 3 plots.

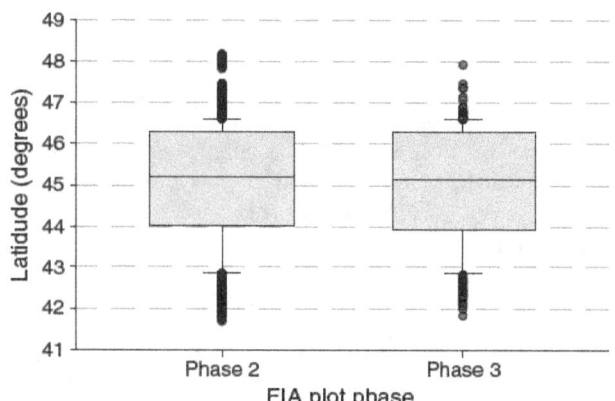

Figure 4.2—Latitudes of phase 2 and phase 3 plots.

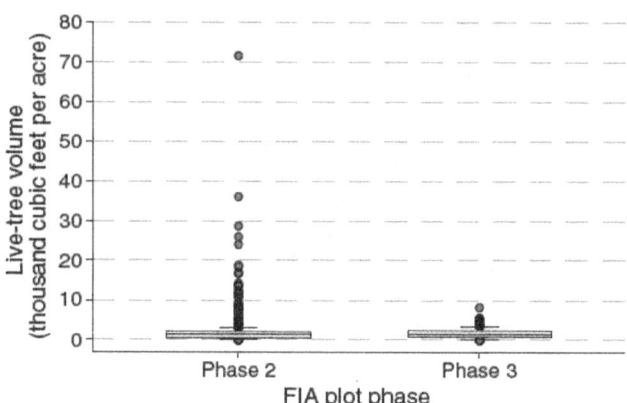

Figure 4.3—Live-tree volume for phase 2 and phase 3 plots.

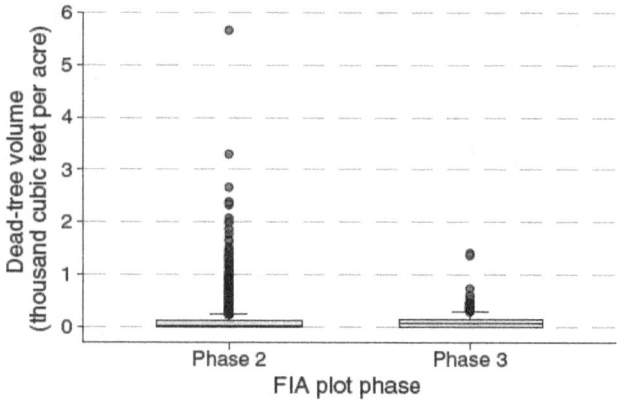

Figure 4.4—Dead-tree volume for phase 2 and phase 3 plots.

Using the target variable mean to estimate the total assumes a horizontal relationship between the target variable and the predictor variables, the ratio estimator (Cochran 1977 chapter 6) and the regression estimator (Cochran 1977 chapter 7) both assume a relatively linear relationship between the target variable and the predictor variables. The only way to know with certainty which assumption is correct would be to implement the P3 protocols on some of the P2 plots with predictor variable values outside the range found on the P3 plots, which may be outside the capabilities of most data users.

Within-Plot Correlation

Why it is a problem

FIA's estimation procedures assumes that a systematic sample of P2 plots can be treated as a simple random sample (Reams and others 2005), and therefore plot-level values can be treated as independent. But the stand-level variables cannot be assumed to be independent *a priori*. Because the variance of the sum of two variables is the variance of one variable plus the variance of the second variable plus two times the covariance, if the target variable values are uncorrelated then the covariance term drops out. However, having correlated target variable values causes calculating the correct variance term to become difficult. Therefore, having uncorrelated stand-level target variables is strongly recommended before using the stand-level values to esti-mate population values. There are a sufficient number of ways that two stands on a plot can interact, that an *a priori* assumption that the target variable values of the two stands on a plot are uncorrelated is inappropriate.

Stand-Level Approaches

One of the standard ways of handling the potential correla-tion between stands is to use plot-level values. For example, Woodall and Monleon (2008) used plot-level values for their population estimate of CWD_c using just P3 plots. The basic component they use in their population estimation equations for CWD_c (y_{hid}) is calculated in their equation 3.1.

$$y_{hid} = \frac{c(\pi/2)}{12L\bar{p}_h^{CWD}} \sum_{j=1}^{4} \sum_{m=1}^{3} \sum_{t} \frac{y_{hijmt}\delta_{hijmtd}}{l_{hijmt}}$$

where

y = the attribute of interest,
l = the length of the CWD piece,

δ = an indicator variable for the domain of interest, c is a constant used to convert to the proper units,

L = the length of a transect in feet (24), and

$\bar{p}_h^{CWD}$ adjusts for parts of plots being outside the population of interest, with the following subscripts: h indicates stratum, i indicates plot, j indicates subplot, m indicates transect, t indicates coarse woody debris piece, and d indicates domain of interest. Using the plot-level values, such as y_{hid}, in the equations for estimating population values allows Woodall and Monleon to avoid having to deal with the issue of within-plot correlations.

If both the target variable and the predictor variables have reasonable plot-level summaries, then conducting the analysis on the plot-level summaries is recommended. Chapter 5 has some suggestions on possible approaches. However, some variables don't lend themselves to a plot-level summary. One example is stand age. The main plot-level summary and average stand age, might not convey the information you wish. Other examples of predictor variables that might not be conducive to plot-level summary values include the presence of harvesting and forest type. When either the target variable or one of the predictor variables does not lend itself to a plot-level summary variable, using stand-level variable may have to be used and the problem of correlations between values from different stands on the same plot will need to be addressed.

Testing for Correlated Stand Values

The main tests for correlation between two variables are the Pearson's correlation coefficient, and the Spearman's rank correlation coefficient. The formula for the Pearson's correlation coefficient is

$$r = \frac{\sum (x_i - \bar{x})(y_i - \bar{y})}{\left(\sum (x_i - \bar{x})^2\right)^{0.5} \left(\sum (y_i - \bar{y})^2\right)^{0.5}}$$

For the purposes of testing for correlations between target variable values of different stands on a plot, x is the target variable value for one stand on plot i and y is the target variable value from a different stand on plot i. The significance tests for Pearson's correlation coefficient is designed for target variables that are normally distributed. Since many target variables have skewed distributions, most target variables should not be assumed to be normally distributed. Spearman's rank correlation coefficient uses the same formula as the Pearson's correlation coefficient, except that instead of using the target variable values, the ranks of the

target variable values are used. Under the hypothesis that the true correlation is zero, for both correlation $t = r\sqrt{\frac{n-2}{1-r^2}}$ coefficients follows a t distribution with (n-2) degrees of freedom. Most statistical software packages will calculate the p-values.

This significance test is different from the significance tests usually run during statistical analysis. The usual null hypothesis is that the correlation is zero and the usual objective is to prove that the correlation is not zero. However, in this case, the null hypothesis is that the correlation is not zero and the objective is to prove that the correlation is zero. Usually the goal is to find a p-value of ≤ 0.05. In this case, the goal is to find both p-values >0.20.

Example 1: Linear Regression

The segmented linear regression model in chapter 3 generates a set of issues beyond the correlation problem. To be able to concentrate on the correlation problem, another linear regression was run without any segmentation. The target variable is CWD_c in tons-per-acre and the predictor variables are stand age, harvesting, volume of dead trees, volume of live trees, latitude, and soil moisture class indicator variables. The predictor variables with parameter estimates that are significantly different from zero are stand age, volume of dead trees, harvesting, and the mesic soil moisture indicator. This regression equation has an R-squared value of 0.287 and a mean square error of 3.649. The variables with their parameter values are shown in table 4.1.

Table 4.1—Linear regression variables and parameters

Variable	Parameter estimates	p-value
Intercept	-0.18948	0.6031
Stand age	0.01322	0.0062
Volume of dead trees (*cubic feet per acre*)	0.00581	0.0001
Harvesting	1.82534	0.0005
Mesic soil moisture indicator	0.61513	0.0193

The values used to test for correlations between multiple stands on a single plot are the regression residuals. Of the 247 plots with forested stands, 34 have more than 1 forested stand, with 1 plot having 3 forested stands. Once the regression equation was fit to the full dataset, 2 residuals were randomly chosen from the 34 plots with more than 1 forested stand (fig. 4.5). The Pearson correlation coefficient

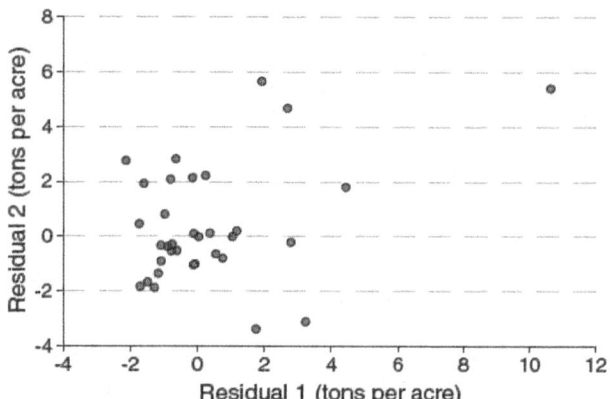

Figure 4.5—Residuals from nonsegmented regression equation.

is 0.386 with a *p*-value of 0.024, and the Spearman rank correlation coefficient is 0.181 with a *p*-value of 0.306. Since the *p*-value for the Pearson correlation coefficient is <0.20, the residuals should not be considered to be uncorrelated. Therefore, using the stand-level data to estimate population totals using this equation is inappropriate.

If the residuals were uncorrelated the approach would be to multiply the regression estimator for CWD_c per forest acre from the P3 plots by the forest area estimate from the P2 plots. Both the estimate for CWD_c per forest acre and the estimate of forest area are random variables. Goodman (1960) derived the formula for the estimated variance of a product of two independent random variables as

$$V(x_1 x_2)/n_G = V(x_1)\bar{x}_2^2/n_G \\ + \bar{x}_1^2 V(x_2)/n_G \\ - V(x_1)V(x_2)/n_G^2 \quad (4.1)$$

where

V = variance,

n_G = number of observations.

Our first random variable is the regression estimate of the amount of CWD_c per acre within the whole population. The regression estimator does require that the relationship between the predictor variables and the target variable is approximately linear and that the variance around the regression line is fairly constant across the ranges of the predictor variables (Cochran 1977). In this example, both requirements are highly questionable. Cochran's equation 7.24 gives the formula for the linear regression estimator as

$$\bar{y}_{lr} \quad \bar{y} + \sum b(\bar{X} \quad \bar{x}) \quad (4.2)$$

where

$-$ = the mean CWD_c per acre from the P3 plots,

b = the vector of parameter estimates,

$\bar{X}$ are the predictor variable means from the P2 plots,

$\bar{x}$ = predictor variable means from the P3 plots. The means for the CWD_c and the predictor variables appear in table 4.2.

Table 4.2—Stand-level means from P3 and P2 plots

Variable	P3 mean	P2 mean
CWD_c	1.7907	
Stand age	61.0645161	56.2802917
Volume of dead trees *(cubic feet per acre)*	111.21186	86.27300
Harvesting	0.060484	0.058594
Mesic soil moisture indicator	0.67742	0.69468

P3 = Phase 3; P2 = Phase 2; CWD_c = coarse wood debris carbon.

The regression estimator $(\bar{y}_{lr})$ is 1.589752 tons per acre. Ignoring the finite population correction factor, Cochran's formula for the variance of the regression estimator becomes

$$\frac{1}{n(n-p)} \sum_{i=1}^{n} (e_i - \bar{e})^2 \quad (4.3)$$

For this linear regression example, the variance is 0.014714.

As with the standard population estimation procedure for CWD_c, the P2 forest area estimation procedure starts with calculating plot level totals (Scott and others 2005). The forest area estimation procedure starts with Scott and others' equation 4.1,

$$P_{hid} = \frac{\sum_j^4 \sum_k^{K_{hij}} a_{mhijk} \delta_{hijkd}}{a_m \bar{P}_{mh}}$$

where a_m is mapped area, δ is an indicator function, h is the subscript for stratum, j is the subscript for subplot, i is the subscript for plot, k is the subscript for condition, d is the subscript for domain, and $\bar{P}_{mh}$ is an adjustment factor for portions of plots outside of the population. Scott and others' equation for the stratum mean (4.3) is

$$\bar{P}_{hd} = \frac{\sum_i^{n_h} P_{hid}}{n_h},$$

and their equation for the variance of the stratum mean (4.4) is

$$V(\bar{P}_{hd}) = \frac{\sum_i^{n_h} P_{hid}^2 - n_h \bar{P}_{hd}^2}{n_h(n_h - 1)}.$$

Since Michigan currently uses satellite imagery to create their stratification, the estimate for the total forested area (Scott and others 2005, equation 4.5) is

$$\hat{A}_d = A_T \sum_h^H W_h \overline{P_{hd}} = A_T \overline{P_d}$$

where $\hat{A}$ is the estimated area in the domain (forested), A_T is the total area, W_h are the stratum weights, and $\overline{P_d}$ is the weighted average of the proportion of the area in the domain (forest). The estimate of the variance for the estimated area in the domain (forested) (Scott and others 2005, equation 4.6) is

$$\left(\hat{A}_d\right) = \frac{A_T^2}{n}\left[\sum_h^H W_h n_h V\left(\overline{P_{hd}}\right) + \sum_h^H \left(1 - W_n\right)\frac{n_h}{n} V\left(\overline{P_{hd}}\right)\right].$$

Table 4.3 contains the values used to estimate the forest area and its variance using the P2 data and the results.

Table 4.3—Parameter values used to estimate forest area and its variance using P2 plot data

Stratum	W_h	n_h	$\overline{P_{hd}}$	$v(\overline{P_{hd}})$
1	0.39784	5,636	0.7485	0.05556
2	0.11982	1,583	0.44816	0.19384
3	0.06562	888	0.72197	0.15401
4	0.16553	2,270	0.85128	0.09843
5	0.25119	3,490	0.88295	0.08495

P2 = Phase 2.

The last parameter in Goodman's equation for the variance of a product of random variables is n_G, which is the number of joint observations. There is one estimate of CWD_c per acre, and one estimate of forest area, therefore the number of observations is one. The parameter values for Goodman's variance of the product of two random variables appear in table 4.4. The estimated total amount of CWD_c is 29,186,836.45 tons. The variance of this estimate is $V(\hat{CWD}_{c_{lr}}) = 1.2022 * 10^{14}$.

Segmented Linear Regression

The segments in the segmented linear regression equation used in chapter 3 increases the complexity. The segments can be treated as a second stratification based on stand characteristics. The strata are designed to match the linear regression segments. Using the chapter 3 segmented regression equation as an example, the three strata would be stands that have had a harvesting treatment, stands <30 years old that have not had a harvesting treatment, and stands ≥30 years old that have not had a harvesting treatment. The sizes of these strata are not known in advance, so double sampling for stratification will need to be used. Double sampling for stratification will use the P2 plots to estimate the proportion of stands within each stratum, along with the relationship between P3 stand variables and P2 stand variables to estimate the average CWD_c per acre for each stratum. The estimated stratum means are then averaged by weight to create the overall stratified mean and the Cochran's equation for calculating the variance for double sampling for stratification. The stratified mean and variance are then combined with the P2 forest area estimates in the same manner as the regression estimator in the previous example.

The first step after fitting the initial equations is to test for correlations between stands on the same plot. The residuals from all of the regression segments need to be calculated. Then the residuals from plots with more than one stand are randomly divided into two groups and tested for correlation. The graph of the pairs of residuals (fig. 4.6) shows a clear pattern of correlation. Both the Pearson's and Spearman's correlation coefficients agree with the visual assessment. The Pearson's correlation coefficient is 0.606 with a p-value of <0.0001, and the Spearman's correlation coefficient is 0.366 with a p-value of 0.0125. Therefore, this segmented regression equation should not be used to estimate the total amount of CWD_c in Michigan with this data set.

Table 4.4—Parameters used to calculate the variance of the linear regression estimate of CWD_c per acre using Goodman's formula

Parameter	$\overline{y}_{lr}$ CWD$_c$ per acre	$v(\overline{y}_{lr})$ Variance of CWD$_c$ per acre	$\hat{A}_d$ Forest area	$v(\hat{A}_d)$ Variance of forest area	n_G Number of "observed" estimates
			- - - acres - - -		
Value	1.589752	0.014714	18,359,364.51	2.8109*10^{13}	1

CWD$_c$ = coarse wood debris carbon.

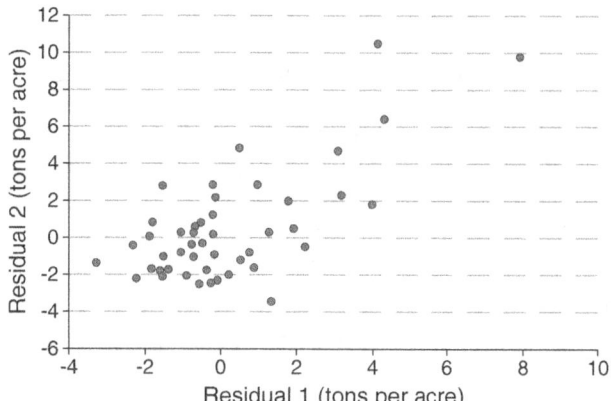

Figure 4.6—Residuals from segment linear regression.

The current objective is to demonstrate how the segmented regression equation could be used to estimate the amount of CWD_c in forests in Michigan. Therefore the segmented regression equation will continue, despite the fact that it failed the within-plot correlation criteria. Each of the strata means CWD_c are estimated along with its variance. For the harvested stands, the model is the mean (3.282 tons per acre) and the variance of the harvested stands is 10.4040. Therefore the variance of the mean is 10.4040 divided by 15 or 0.69360.

For both the young unharvested stands and the older harvested stands, the model is a linear regression function. The estimated mean for these strata are found using equation 4.2, with it variance found in equation 4.3. The parameter estimates for the unharvested young stands appear in table 4.5, and the variable means for unharvested young stands on P2 and P3 plots appear in table 4.6. The estimated mean of the unharvested young stands is 1.4283804. The variance of the mean CWD_c in unharvested young stands is 0.09338.

Table 4.5—Linear regression results for young unharvested stands: segmented model

Variable	Parameter estimate	p-value
Intercept	3.38914	0.0003
Stand age	-0.11600	0.0088
Mean square error	2.61452	
Number of observations	28	

Table 4.6—Stand level P3 and P2 means for young unharvested stands

Variable	P3 mean	P2 mean
CWD_c	1.2721429	
Stand age	18.2500	16.9031250

P3 = Phase 3; P2 = Phase 2; CWD_c = coarse wood debris carbon.

The parameter estimates for the unharvested older stands appear in table 4.7, and the variable means for the unharvested older stands on P2 and P3 plots appear in table 4.8. The estimated mean CWD_c in unharvested older stands is 1.660813. The variance of the estimated mean CWD_c in unharvested older stands is 0.01734.

Table 4.7—Linear regression results for older unharvested stands: segmented model

Variable	Parameter estimate	p-value
Intercept	-0.84527	0.0769
Stand age	0.02200	0.0003
Volume of dead trees	0.00569	0.0001
Mesic soil indicator	0.79980	0.0052
Mean square error	3.81585	
Number of observations	220	

Table 4.8—Stand level P3 and P2 means for older unharvested stands

Variable	P3 mean	P2 mean
CWD_c	1.8567273	
Stand age	66.5136364	63.0324828
Volume of dead trees	121.8897219	99.6288692
Mesic soil indicator	0.6818182	0.6893124

P3 = Phase 3; P2 = Phase 2; CWD_c = coarse wood debris carbon.

The results from the 3 segments combined using Cochran's equations for double sampling for stratification. The formula (Cochran 1977, equation 12.1) for the mean is,

$$\overline{CWD}_{st} = \sum_{h=1}^{H} w_h \overline{CWD}_h$$

where W_h is the stratum weight for stratum h. In this example, I am using the ratio of the number of stands within each stratum on the P2 plots to the total number of stands on the P2 plots as ____. Because the true proportion of the different segments in the population are not known, but rather estimated from the P2 plots, the variance formula for double sampling for stratification needs to be used. Ignoring the finite population correction factor and using the notation in this example Cochran's equation for the variance from double sampling for stratification (12.32) is

$$\sum_h \left(\frac{n'_h}{n'} \frac{1}{1} \right) \frac{w_h s_h^2}{n_h} + \frac{1}{(n'-1)} \sum_h w_h \left(\overline{CWD_{c_{st}}} - \overline{CWD_{c_h}} \right)^2 ,$$

where n'_h is the number of stands on P2 plots in the stratum, is the number of stands on P2 plots, and n_h is the number of n' stands on the P3 plots in the stratum. The values used to calculate the stratified mean and its variance appear in table 4.9.

The estimated CWD_c per acre using the stratification base on the stand-level data, $(\overline{CWD_{c_{st}}})$ and its variance can then be combined with the P2 forest area estimate and its variance to create an estimate of the total amount of CWD_c using Goodman's formula for the variance of the product of two random variables in the same manner as with the non-segmented linear equation example. The values used to calculate the total amount of CWD_c and its variance using Goodman's formula (equation 4.1) appear in table 4.10. The estimate of the total CWD_c is $\widehat{CWD}_{c_{st}} = 3.2408*10^7$ tons of carbon. The estimated variance of the total CWD_c is $V\left(\overline{CWD_{c_{st}}} \right) = 9.3172*10^{13}$ tons squared.

Conclusions

Eventually, a choice has to be made: whether to estimate population totals using stand- or plot-level data. While there is some instinctive appeal in analyzing the data at the stand level, the data range and within plot correlation requirements may make analyzing the data at the stand level impossible. Within-plot correlations can be created by shared local variations in any of a large number of variables, such as soil conditions, moisture, or disturbance history. The large number of possible causes of shared local variation suggests that finding no within-plot correlations unlikely and most analysis will have to be done at the plot level.

Table 4.9—Strata values used to calculate stratified estimate of mean CWD$_c$ and its estimated variance

Stratum	n'_h (Number of P2 observations)	$\overline{CWD_{c_h}}$ (estimated mean CWD$_c$)	$v\left(\overline{CWD_{c_h}} \right)$ (variance of the estimated mean CWD$_c$)
Harvested	707	3.282	0.69360
Unharvested young	160	1.4283	0.09338
Unharvested older	9,759	1.6608	0.01734
Total	10,626	1.7652 $(\overline{CWD_{c_{st}}})$	0.01808 $v(\overline{CWD_{c_{st}}})$

CWD$_c$ = coarse wood debris carbon; P2 = Phase 2.

Table 4.10—Parameters used to calculate the variance of the segmented linear regression estimate of CWD$_c$ per acre using Goodman's formula

Parameter	$(\overline{CWD_{c_{st}}})$ CWD$_c$ per acre	$v(\overline{CWD_{c_{st}}})$ Variance of CWD$_c$ per acre	$\hat{A}_d$ Forest area	$v\left(\hat{A}_d \right)$ Variance of forest area	n_G Number of "observed" estimates
			- - - acres - - -		
Value	1.7652	0.01808	18,359,364.51	$2.8109 * 10^{13}$	1

CWD$_c$ = coarse wood debris carbon.

Literature Cited

Barbour, M.G.; Burk, J.H.; Pitts, W.D. 1987. Terrestrial plant ecology, 2nd ed. Menlo Park, CA: The Benjamin/Cummings Publishing Co., Inc. 636 p.

Cochran, W.G. 1977. Sampling techniques. 3rd ed. New York City, NY: John Wiley and Sons. 428 p.

Goodman: L.A. 1960. On the exact variance of products. Journal of the American Statistical Association. University of Chicago: 55(292): 708–713.

Reams, G.A.; Smith, W.D.; Hansen, M.H. [and others]. 2005. The forest inventory and analysis sampling frame. In: Bechtold, W.A.; Patterson, P.L., eds. The enhanced forest inventory and analysis program—national sampling design and estimation procedures. Gen. Tech. Rep. SRS–80. Asheville, NC: U.S. Department of Agriculture Forest Service, Southern Research Station. 11–26.

Scott, C.T.; Bechtold, W.A.; Reams, G.A. [and others]. 2005. Sample-based estimators used by the forest inventory and analysis national information management system. In: Bechtold, W.A.; Patterson, P.L., eds. The enhanced forest inventory and analysis program—national sampling design and estimation procedures. Gen. Tech. Rep. SRS–80. Asheville, NC: U.S. Department of Agriculture Forest Service, Southern Research Station. 43–67.

Woodall, C.W.; Monleon, V. J. 2008. Sampling protocol, estimation, and analysis procedures for the down woody materials indicator of the FIA program. Gen. Tech. Rep. NRS–22, Newtown Square, PA: U.S. Department of Agriculture Forest Service, Northern Research Station. 68 p.

Chapter 5: Estimation Using Double Sampling for Regression

James Westfall

In most large-area forest inventories, sample intensity and plot measurement effort must be balanced within the context of a finite amount of available resources. For a given allowable expenditure, the sample size can be increased if the number of attributes measured on each plot is decreased, and vice-versa (Kangas and Maltamo 2006). A good example is the Forest Inventory and Analysis (FIA) program of the U.S. Forest Service. Due to the relatively high costs of obtaining forest health indicator information (e.g., down woody materials, soil properties, understory vegetation), these data are collected on only a small subset of the overall sample (Reams and others 2005). As such, analysts are faced with reporting estimates of forest health attributes at large spatial scales in order to obtain sample sizes that provide an acceptable level of precision.

This limited sample size/plot effort dilemma has resulted in the adoption of alternative strategies to improve the precision of estimates. Double sampling involves measuring 'high-cost' variables on only a subset of the sample plots and taking advantage of the correlations between these variables and common mensuration variables collected on all plots (Schreuder and others 1993). These relationships must be developed from the smaller subset of the plots, where both the attribute of interest and auxiliary information are available. A common technique is to use a simple linear regression model, however, multiple linear regression models can also be employed. The double sampling estimate is equivalent to using the predicted values where the 'high-cost' variable is missing (Chojnacky and others 2004, Coble and Grogan 2007). The reduction in the standard error of the estimate depends on the strength of the correlation as measured by the regression model (R^2) (Cochran 1977).

Another approach to increasing the precision of estimates is stratification. In stratified sampling, the units of the population are subdivided into strata where the units within strata have similar observed values. This often results in precise estimates for each stratum that can then be combined into a precise estimate for the entire population (Cochran 1977). The efficacy of stratification is exhibited by wide use of the technique in forest inventory. In the United States, stratification has been used for decades by the FIA program (Reams and others. 2005). Similarly, national forest inventories in Sweden (Nilsson and others 2005), Finland (Katila and others 2000), Switzerland (Köhl 2001), and Canada (Gillis 2001) implement stratification strategies as part of the inventory design.

In this chapter, the double sampling for regression technique will be used to illustrate how sample estimates can be improved via incorporation of auxiliary information. First, the traditional application of a double sampling regression estimator is used to outline the underlying methods and evaluate the efficacy of such an approach. However, this classical approach is limited in utility due to the simple linear model. Thus, a more complex regression model that better fits the data is also presented. This increased explanatory ability translates into further improvements in the precision of the estimate. The effectiveness of stratification in conjunction with the regression estimator was also evaluated.

Data

The data used in this paper are those described in the introductory text. As a brief reminder to readers, phase 1 is the post-stratification effort where each plot is assigned to 1 of 5 strata based on mapped canopy cover classes (table 5.1). There were 13,274 phase 2 (P2) plots having data on a range of tree- and site-level variables such as tree species, tree height, site index, forest type, etc. The phase 3 (P3) subset of 381 plots also contains data for coarse woody debris carbon (CWD_c). On nonforested areas, CWD_c is not measured and is assumed to be zero. On forested conditions, CWD_c is >0 when 1 or more CWD_c pieces are measured and $CWD_c = 0$ otherwise.

Table 5.1—Summary of post-stratification for Michigan

Stratum	Canopy cover	Weight (w_h)
	- percent -	
1	0–5	0.39784
2	6–50	0.11982
3	51–65	0.06562
4	66–80	0.16553
5	81–100	0.25119

Section 1—Classical Double Sampling for Regression

Methods

Perhaps the most straightforward method of improving estimates of CWD_c via correlations with P2 variables is double sampling for regression. In the traditional application of this method, the correlation between CWD_c and a P2 variable is established using the P3 plot data through a simple linear regression model:

where:

$$C\hat{W}D_{cj} = \hat{\beta}_0 + \hat{\beta}_1 x_j \qquad [5.1]$$

CWD_{cj} = predicted coarse woody debris carbon (tons per acre) on plot j

x_j = P2 variable correlated with CWD_c on plot j

$\hat{\beta}_0 + \hat{\beta}_1$ = parameters estimated from the data

Additional information needed to compute the double sampling for regression estimates are the mean CWD_c from the smaller P3 sample, $\overline{(CWD_c)}$, the mean of x_j from the larger P2 sample $(\overline{\chi}')$, and the mean of x_j from the P3 sample $(\overline{\chi})$. The regression estimate $\overline{CWD}_{cr}$ is the $\overline{CWD}_c$ adjusted for differences between the large and small sample means of x_j:

$$\overline{CWD}_{cr} = \overline{CWD}_c + \beta_1(\overline{x}' - \overline{x}) \qquad [5.2]$$

The estimated variance requires both the large (n') and small (n) sample sizes, the number of units in the population (N), as well as other computed quantities (Cochran 1977):

$$V(\overline{CWD}_{cr}) = \frac{S^2_{\text{CWD}_{c.x}}}{n}$$
$$+ \frac{S^2_{\text{CWD}_c} - S^2_{\text{CWD}_{c.x}}}{n'} - \frac{S^2_{\text{CWD}_c}}{N} \qquad [5.3]$$

where:

$$s^2_{\text{CWDc x}} \quad \frac{1}{n \; 2}$$

$$\left[\sum_{j=1}^{n} (CWD_{cj} - \overline{CWD})^2 \right. \qquad [5.4]$$

$$\left. - \beta_1^2 \sum_{j=1}^{n} (x_j \quad \overline{x})^2 \right]$$

$$s^2_{\text{CWD}_c} \quad \frac{\sum_{j=1}^{n}(CWD_{cj} \quad \overline{CWD})^2}{n \; 1} \qquad [5.5]$$

Estimation of the population total $C\hat{W}D_c$ and associated standard error $SE(C\hat{W}D_c)$ derives from multiplication by the known total area of the population (A_T):

$$C\hat{W}D_c = A_T \overline{CWD}_{cr} \qquad [5.6]$$

$$V\left(C\hat{W}D_c\right) = A_T^2 V(\overline{CWD}_{cr}) \qquad [5.7]$$

$$SE\left(C\hat{W}D_c\right) = \sqrt{A_T^2 V(\overline{CWD}_{cr})} \qquad [5.8]$$

Additional precision can likely be obtained by applying the double sampling design to a stratified population. For typical large-area forest inventories where plot locations are fixed in advance, the population is usually post-stratified. If the β_1 estimates differ among the h strata, the appropriate methodology is to compute estimates of $(\overline{CWD}_{cr})$ and $V(\overline{CWD}_{cr})$ within each stratum (Cochran 1977). These stratum-level estimates are then combined using the stratum weight information to obtain the population total $C\hat{W}D_{cs}$. The estimated variance $V(C\hat{W}D_{cs})$ takes into account the additional randomness associated with post-stratified stratum sample sizes (Scott and others 2005):

$$C\hat{W}D_{cs} = A_T \sum_{i \; 1}^{h} W_h \overline{CWD}_{crh} \qquad [5.9]$$

$$V\left(C\hat{W}D_{cs}\right) = \frac{A_T^2}{n}\left[\sum_{i \; 1}^{h} W_h n_h V\left(\overline{CWD}_{crh}\right) \right.$$
$$\left. + \sum_{i \; 1}^{h}(1 \quad W_h)\frac{n_h}{n} V(\overline{CWD}_{crh}) \right] \qquad [5.10]$$

where

W_h = weight for stratum h

n_h = number of sample plots in stratum h

$\overline{CWD}_{crh}$ = regression estimate of $\overline{CWD}_{cr}$ in stratum h

$V(\overline{CWD}_{crh})$ = variance of $\overline{CWD}_{cr}$ in stratum h.

Results/Discussion

A number of P2 variables were assessed for degree of correlation with CWD_c, with standing dead tree biomass (D_B)having the highest correlation of those evaluated. However, it was noted that there were two values of D_B that were much larger than the other data points (outliers). To minimize the effect of these extreme observations and obtain a better model fit, the square root of D_B was used as the predictor variable in the regression. The relevant statistics for CWD_c and $\sqrt{D_B}$ are reported in table 5.2. Using these statistics and the linear regression results (table 5.3), the calculated value of $\widehat{CWD}_c$ was 30,504,473 tons with $SE(\widehat{CWD}_c)$ of 2,658,317 tons. In comparison, the estimate using only the P3 plots was 34,628,709 tons with the standard error of the estimate being 3,199,258 tons. The smaller mean value of D_B in the larger sample resulted in a decrease in the estimate of $\widehat{CWD}_c$. Taking advantage of the correlation between CWD_c and D_B produced a 17 percent decrease in $SE(\widehat{CWD}_c)$.

Using data from post-stratification (tables 5.2, 5.3), the regression estimates were calculated independently within each stratum. The within-strata adjustments provided increases or decreases to having direction and size depending on the sign and magnitude of the difference between $\sqrt{D_B}$ and $\sqrt{D_B'}$. The estimates were then combined across strata for an estimate of the population total $\widehat{CWD}_{cs}$ of 31,391,701 tons with an associated $SE(\widehat{CWD}_{cs})$ of 2,615,489 tons. The combined effect of post-stratification and the use of D_B information resulted in a decrease in the standard error from 3,199,258 to 2,615,489 tons (18 percent). The use of post-stratification alone resulted in a modest 1-percent decrease relative to the standard error obtained using the regression estimator. The ineffectiveness of the stratification was mostly due to several within-stratum variances being higher than that of the unstratified sample. This was likely due to the stratification being based on remotely-sensed canopy cover information, which may not correlate well with amounts of CWD_c on the ground. Further increases in precision could be obtained using an alternative source of stratification information that better categorizes plots having similar amounts of CWD_c.

Readers may have noted that in addition to the changes in standard error resulting from the various techniques, the estimated values of population total also fluctuate. While the estimators used in this study are unbiased, differing

Table 5.2—Summary statistics for entire sample and by stratum

Stratum	$\overline{CWD}_c$	$S^2_{CWD_c}$	$S^2_{CWD_{c.x}}$	$\sqrt{D_B}$	$\sqrt{D_B'}$	n	n'	N
All	0.931	2.818	1.954	38.5	32.2	381	13,274	223,189,644
1	0.144	1.073	0.635	4.8	2.9	160	5,537	88,793,768
2	0.482	1.246	0.857	29.9	24.6	37	1,500	26,742,583
3	1.263	2.476	1.507	69.2	46.2	25	837	14,645,704
4	1.636	3.254	2.913	67.6	65.7	64	2,121	36,944,582
5	1.869	3.896	3.643	70.7	60.2	95	3,279	56,063,007

Note: Population area (A_T) = 37,198,274 acres.

Table 5.3—Parameter estimates (with standard errors) and fit statistics for simple linear regression of CWD_c on $\sqrt{D_B}$ for entire sample and by stratum

Stratum	β_0	β_1	R^2	RMSE
All	0.2450 (0.0890)	0.01784 (0.0014)	0.308	1.954
1	0.0258 (0.0640)	0.02457 (0.0023)	0.412	0.635
2	0.0469 (0.1845)	0.01454 (0.0035)	0.332	0.857
3	-0.3971 (0.4773)	0.02400 (0.0059)	0.417	1.507
4	0.7945 (0.3610)	0.01245 (0.0043)	0.119	2.913
5	1.1821 (0.3179)	0.00971 (0.0035)	0.075	3.643

results can be obtained if different samples are used, e.g., P2 vs. P3. This phenomenon is the theoretical basis for calculating uncertainty statistics such as standard errors. Also, the implementation of stratification can affect results depending on the proportional distribution of plots to strata. This can be a concern if the number of plots in a stratum deviates substantially from the expected number based on the stratum area (Coulston 2008); however, there was close agreement in this study such that stratification had little impact on the estimates of amounts of CWD_c. As such, the fluctuations in estimates shown here are expected to occur.

Section 2—Double Sampling for Regression (Zero-inflated Gamma)

Methods

A review of the data indicates 168 of the 381 plots are nonforest and by definition have $CWD_c = 0$. Thus, the data are zero-inflated, i.e., there are multiple data points where the value is zero. When this type of data is encountered in a regression analysis, a zero-inflated modeling approach is often used (El-Shaarawi and Piegorsch 2002). For continuous variables, zero-inflated gamma (ZIG) models are usually employed (Feuerverger 1979). These models consist of a mixture of two distributions: a point mass distribution at zero, and a gamma distribution.

Gamma distributions are described by two parameters,

$$X \sim Gamma(\alpha, \beta)$$

where α is the shape parameter and β is the scale parameter. The mean of the distribution is $\alpha\beta$. For more detailed information on gamma distributions, see Balakrishnan and Nevzorov (2003).

To implement the ZIG model, we differentiate between assumed zeros due to nonforest status and observed values on forested plots where no CWD pieces were sampled. To conduct the analyses, a logistic regression model is employed in which the response variable is binary, i.e., 1 for no CWD pieces and 0 when one or more CWD pieces sampled. The purpose of the logistic regression model is to estimate the probability that a given plot has $CWD_c = 0$.

$$\Pr(CWD_{cj} = 0)$$
$$= \frac{1}{1 + \exp(-(\hat{\varphi}_0 + \hat{\varphi}_1 NF_j))} \qquad [5.11]$$

where

$$\Pr(CWD_{cj} = 0) = \text{probability plot } j \text{ has } CWD_c = 0$$

NF_j = proportion of plot j that is nonforest

$(\hat{\varphi}_0, \hat{\varphi}_1)$ = parameters to be estimated from the data

The CWD_c values from forested plots were modeled as a gamma response. To accommodate the gamma distribution, zero values were assigned a value slightly larger than zero (1E-8).

$$C\hat{W}D_{cj} \sim Gamma\left(\frac{\hat{\beta}_0 + \hat{\beta}_1 x_{1j} + \hat{\beta}_2 x_{2j}}{\hat{\theta}}, \hat{\theta}\right) \qquad [5.12]$$

where

$C\hat{W}D_{cj}$ = predicted coarse woody debris carbon (tons per acre) on plot j

x_{1j}, x_{2j} = P2 variables correlated with CWD_c on plot j

$\hat{\beta}_0, \hat{\beta}_1, \hat{\beta}_2, \hat{\theta}$ = parameters estimated from the data

Note that the parameterization of [5.12] results in the mean of the distribution being equal to the numerator of the shape parameter. Using the model results, amounts of $C\hat{W}D_{cj}$ were assigned to plots where CWD_c data were not collected. First, the probability of $CWD_{cj} = 0$ was assessed using [5.11]. Plots having probability of >0.5 were given a value of $C\hat{W}D_{cj} = 0$. For the remaining plots, values of $C\hat{W}D_{cj}$ based on [5.12] were used.

Estimation of population totals—The advantage of using auxiliary information is illustrated using the estimation procedures described by Scott and others. (2005). In this example, an estimate of the total amount of CWD_c in the population is desired. From the analysis above, each plot has a corresponding value of CWD_{cj}. To account for potential sampling bias associated with portions of plots that occur outside the population boundary, each plot value must be divided by the mean proportion of mapped plot area falling within the population:

$$\bar{p}_m = \sum_{j=1}^{n} \frac{a_{mj}}{a_j n} \qquad [5.13]$$

$$CWD_{cj'} = \frac{CWD_{cj}}{\bar{p}_m} \qquad [5.14]$$

where

a_{mj} = area of plot j within the population
a_j = total area of plot j
$\hat{CWD}_{cj}$ = CWD_{cj} per acre adjusted for plots that overlap the population boundary
$\overline{P}_m$ = mean proportion of mapped plot area falling within the population

In the context of this example, the only plots that may straddle the population boundary would occur at the state borders. It is likely that relatively few plots would meet this criterion, so it will be assumed that $\overline{P}_m \approx 1$ and therefore CWD_{cj}, = CWD_{cj}. It should be noted that this assumption may not hold for other populations that may be either small or fragmented.

To estimate the population total CWD_c, the average of the CWD_{cj} is calculated and multiplied by the area in the population:

$$\hat{CWD}_c = A_T \frac{\sum_{j\ 1}^{n} CWD_{cj}}{n} \qquad [5.15]$$
$$= A_T C\overline{WD}_c$$

where
$\hat{CWD}_c$ = estimated total CWD_c in the population (tons)
n = number of plots in the sample
A_T = known area of the population (acres)

If only the observed data points (381 independent plots) were used for estimation in [5.15], the variance of the total would be computed from:

$$V\left(\hat{CWD}_C\right) = A_T^2 \frac{\sum_{j\ 1}^{n}(CWD_{cj} - C\overline{WD}_c)^2}{n(n-1)} \qquad [5.16]$$

To take advantage of the auxiliary information, it is desirable to use all 13,274 plots in the sample. However, this complicates the computation of the variance as plots having predicted values from the ZIG model are not independent observations and the use of [5.16] would provide an estimate that is too small. Double sampling for regression estimators can be employed when only a subsample of data points have the attribute of interest but the entire sample has useful auxiliary information (Cochran 1977). Khan and Tripathi (1967) provide the variance estimator when multiple linear regression is employed:

$$V_m\left(\hat{CWD}_c\right) = nV\left(\hat{CWD}_c\right)\left(1 - R^2\right)$$
$$\left[\frac{1}{n} + \left(\frac{1}{n} - \frac{1}{n'}\right)\left(\frac{p}{n-p-2}\right)\right] \qquad [5.17]$$
$$+ \frac{nV(\hat{CWD}_c)R^2}{n'}$$

where

p = number of auxiliary variates used in the regression model
R^2 = proportion of variation in CWD_c explained by the regression model
others = as previously defined

If it is reasonable that n is large, n $\approx$ n' or p is small in relation to n such that the second term within brackets ≈ 0, [5.17] can be simplified to:

$$V_m\left(\hat{CWD}_c\right) = V\left(\hat{CWD}_c\right)\left(1 - R^2\right)$$
$$+ \frac{nV\left(\hat{CWD}_c\right)R^2}{n'} \qquad [5.18]$$

This estimator has desirable properties in that 1) when model $R^2 = 0$, no new information has been provided by the model and the estimator reduces to that of the P3 sample, and 2) when model $R^2 = 1$, there is no model error and the estimator reduces to that of the P2 sample.

Estimation on a per-acre basis—While estimates of population totals are informative, it is often of interest to compute estimates on a per-acre-of-forest land basis. This is more complex than estimating a total because an estimate of the area of forest land ($\hat{F}$) is also needed. Additionally, both the estimates of $\hat{CWD}_c$ and $\hat{F}$ are derived from the same plots, so the covariance between the two attributes of interest must be accounted for.

To obtain an estimate (and associated variance) of forest land area, the analyst would use [5.14] – [5.16] above where the variable of interest would be proportion of forest land on each plot (F_i). Given that forest land area proportion is collected on all P2 plots, the entire sample of 13,274 plots can be used to compute the estimate. Using the same assumption as above for [5.14], i.e., $\overline{P}_m = 1$, the total area of forest land ($\hat{F}$) is obtained from [5.15] and the variance of the estimate $V(\hat{F})$ is calculated from [5.16].

As shown by Scott and others (2005), the variance of the per-acre estimate requires that the covariance between $C\hat{W}D_c$ and $\hat{F}$ be computed. This is accomplished via:

$$Cov\left(C\hat{W}D_c,\hat{F}\right) =$$
$$A_T^2 \frac{\sum_{j=1}^{n}\left(CWD_{cj}F_j - nC\bar{W}D_c\bar{F}\right)^2}{n(n-1)} \quad [5.19]$$

Now the estimate of CWD_c per forest land acre, $C\hat{W}D_{ca}$, and associated variance $V(C\hat{W}D_{ca})$ are respectively calculated as

$$C\hat{W}D_{ca} = \frac{C\hat{W}D_c}{\hat{F}} \quad [5.20]$$

$$V\left(C\hat{W}D_{ca}\right) = \frac{1}{\hat{F}^2}\left[V\left(C\hat{W}D_c\right) + C\hat{W}D_{ca}^2 V\left(\hat{F}\right) \right.$$
$$\left. - 2C\hat{W}D_{ca}Cov(C\hat{W}D_c,\hat{F})\right] \quad [5.21]$$

Estimates with post-stratification—Estimation procedures for a post-stratified population are similar to those for a stratified population (Cochran 1977), except that additional estimator variance is incurred due to random sample sizes within strata (Scott and others 2005). For instance, the equations for estimating the population total would be:

$$C\hat{W}D_{cS} = A_T \sum_{i=1}^{h} w_h \frac{\sum_{j=1}^{n_h} CWD_{cjh}}{n_h} \quad [5.22]$$

$$V\left(C\hat{W}D_{cS}\right) = \frac{A_T^2}{n}\left[\sum_{i=1}^{h} w_h n_h V\left(C\hat{W}D_{ch}\right) \right.$$
$$\left. + \sum_{i=1}^{h}(1-w_h)\frac{n_h}{n}V\left(C\hat{W}D_{ch}\right)\right] \quad [5.23]$$

where

$C\hat{W}D_{cS}$ = post-stratified estimated total CWD_c in the population

$V(C\hat{W}D_{cS})$ = variance of post-stratified estimated total CWD_c in the population

w_h = weight for stratum h

$CWD_{cjh} = CWD_c$ on plot j in stratum h

n_h = number of plots in stratum h

Similarly, a post-stratified estimate on a per-acre basis would be calculated from:

$$C\hat{W}D_{caS} = \frac{C\hat{W}D_{cS}}{\hat{F}_S} \quad [5.24]$$

$$V\left(C\hat{W}D_{caS}\right) = \frac{1}{\hat{F}_S^2}\left[V\left(C\hat{W}D_{cS}\right) + C\hat{W}D_{caS}^2 V(\hat{F}_S) \right.$$
$$\left. - 2C\hat{W}D_{caS}Cov(C\hat{W}D_{cS},\hat{F}_S)\right] \quad [5.25]$$

$$Cov\left(C\hat{W}D_{cS},\hat{F}_S\right)$$
$$= \frac{1}{n}\left[\sum_{i=1}^{h} w_h n_h Cov(C\hat{W}D_{ch},\hat{F}_h) \right.$$
$$\left. + \sum_{i=1}^{h}(1-w_h)\frac{n_h}{n}Cov(C\hat{W}D_{ch},\hat{F}_h)\right] \quad [5.26]$$

The within-stratum covariances $Cov(C\hat{W}D_{ch},\hat{F}_h)$ would be computed using the formulation of [5.19]. For all estimates, the standard error is calculated by taking the square root of the estimated variance.

Results

Estimation of total amount—A large number of metrics from P2 data that were possibly correlated with CWD_c were computed. These included various measures such as stand age, stocking, basal area, live- and dead-tree biomass, treatment and disturbance indicators, and site index. Location variables of latitude, longitude, and elevation were also considered. Generally, correlations between these explanatory variables and CWD_c were low, however, $\sqrt{D_B}$ and latitude (decimal degrees) were significant predictors of the gamma distribution parameters for CWD_c on forested plots.

Simultaneous fitting of [5.11] and [5.12] as a system of equations to the 381 P3 plots resulted in an R-squared (R^2) statistic of 0.358 and a root mean-squared error (RMSE) equal to 1.35 (tons per acre). Parameter estimates and their standard errors can be found in table 5.4. For this analysis, model predictions were made for an additional 12,893 plots in Michigan. A comparison between the distributions of the observed and predicted distributions of CWD_c is given in table 5.5. Generally, it is shown that the distribution of predicted values have less variation than the observed data due to the regression model. For instance, both the maximum value and the standard deviation are decreased

Table 5.4—Parameter estimates and standard errors for the ZIG regression model using [5.1] and [5.2]

Parameter	Estimate	Standard error	Pr > |t|
φ_0	-2.58670	0.2711	<0.0001
φ_1	5.80290	0.4803	<0.0001
β_0	-8.14840	2.6478	0.0022
β_1	0.00920	0.0022	<0.0001
β_2	0.20750	0.0596	0.0006
Θ	1.19370	0.1110	<0.0001

ZIG = zero inflated gamma.

Table 5.5—Comparison of distributions of observed CWD_c and predicted CWD_c from the ZIG regression model

Data	n	Minimum	Mean	Maximum	Standard deviation	IQR
Observed	381	0	0.93	11.19	1.68	1.28
Predicted	12,893	0	0.87	5.30	0.92	1.58

CWD_c = coarse woody debris carbon; ZIG = zero inflated gamma; n = number; IQR = interquartile range.

considerably. However, the interquartile range (IQR) of the predicted values was larger than for the observed data. This was due to less skewness in the distribution of predicted values, which resulted in a wider range of values between the 25 and 75 percent quartiles.

Obtaining predicted values of $\widehat{CWD}_{cj}$ from [5.11] and [5.12] for the remaining 12,893 plots where CWD_c was not measured allows for an updated estimate that takes advantage of the correlation between the P2 variables and CWD_c. Using these additional predicted values, the estimate of in $\widehat{CWD}_c$ Michigan was 32,262,427 tons. The standard error of the estimate was 2,583,720 tons. As noted earlier, the estimate using only the 381 P3 plots that were sampled for CWD_c was 34,628,709 tons with a standard error of 3,199,258 tons. A summary of all the estimates and associated standard errors is given in table 5.6.

The inclusion of the predicted values for plots where CWD_c was not measured resulted in a decrease of 2,366,282 tons in the estimate and a reduction in the standard error of 615,538 tons. Even though the sample size increased enormously when the predicted values were included in the sample, the standard error decrease was relatively small. This reflects the weakness of the relationships described by the regression model. Increasing correlations between predictor variables and CWD_c would result in more

Table 5.6—Estimates and standard errors of CWD_c population totals and per acre of forest land for P3 and P2 plot samples, and these same estimates using post-strafication (P3$_s$, P2$_s$)

Basis	CWD_c Total Estimate	CWD_c Total Standard error	CWD_c per acre Estimate	CWD_c per acre Standard error
		tons		
P3	34,628,709	3,199,258	1.849	0.144
P2	32,262,427	2,583,720	1.685	0.116
P3$_s$	34,897,245	2,878,492	1.833	0.143
P2$_s$	33,095,184	2,324,669	1.686	0.115

CWD_c = coarse woody debris carbon; P3 = phase 3; P2 = phase 2; P3$_s$ = phase 3 stratified; P2$_s$ = phase 2 stratified.

substantial improvements in the precision of the estimates. As an example, figure 5.1 depicts the relationship between regression model R^2 and the standard error of $\widehat{CWD}_c$. It is shown that increases in R^2 provide a nonlinear decrease in standard error. For a given increase in R^2, more decrease in standard error is gained at higher values of R^2. In cases where a number of predictor variables are used, adjusted R^2 may be the appropriate measure of correlation, as R^2 will always increase when more explanatory variables are added to the model.

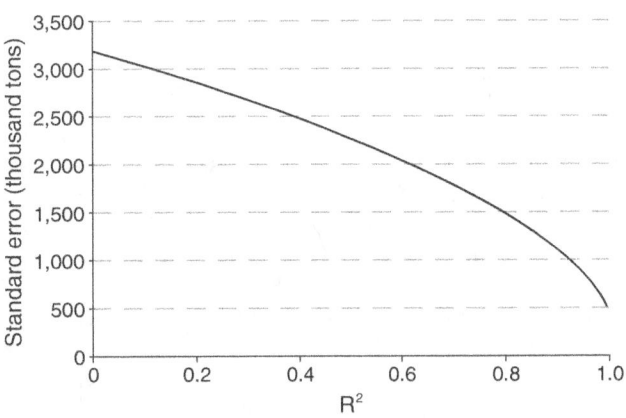

Figure 5.1—Relationship between standard error of $\widehat{CWD}_c$ and R^2 of the regression model.

Estimation of per-acre amount—To establish a baseline from the current sample, estimates of CWD_c on a per-acre-of-forest land basis (denoted $\widehat{CWD}_{ca}$) were computed using the 381 P3 plots. The estimated population total $\widehat{CWD}_c$ and the associated variance $V(\widehat{CWD}_c)$ based on this sample were already computed above. Similar calculations were performed to obtain the estimated area of forest land $(\widehat{F})$ and the variance of the estimate $V(\widehat{F})$. The forest land estimate was 18,731,713 acres with a standard error of 908,065. To obtain all the necessary components for [5.21], the covariance $Cov(\hat{CWD}_c, \hat{F})$ was calculated using [5.19]. Using the values for $\hat{CWD}_c$ and $\hat{F}$ in [5.20], the amount of $\hat{CWD}_{ca}$ is estimated to be 1.849 tons per acre. Using the variance estimated from [5.21], the standard error of the estimate was 0.144 tons per acre.

Estimation using all 13,274 P2 plots in Michigan is accomplished in a similar manner. While the estimate of $\hat{CWD}_c$ results from using predicted values for the remaining 12,893 P2 plots, area of forest land statistics are straightforward as the proportion of forested area (F_j) was recorded on all plots. The area of forest land $\hat{F}$ estimated from the larger sample was 19,141,841 acres with a standard error of 153,257. An estimated $\hat{CWD}_{ca}$ of 1.685 tons per acre was calculated from [5.20]. The standard error of 0.116 tons per acre was calculated by using [5.21] to account for use of the regression model.

Estimation of total amount with post-stratification—To serve as a comparative metric, the post-stratified estimate using only the observed data from P3 plots was calculated. Using the weights developed for the 5 strata, the estimate of $\hat{CWD}_{cS}$ was 34,897,245 tons with a standard error of 2,878,492 tons. The effect of stratification is seen in the reduction of the standard error, which was 3,199,258 tons from the unstratified estimate.

Taking advantage of the predicted values of CWD_c for the 12,893 plots without observed data results in a post-stratified estimated population total of 33,095,184 tons with a standard error of 2,324,669 tons. Thus, the combination of obtaining predicted values where data were missing along with post-stratification resulted in a decrease in the standard error of 874,589 tons (about 27 percent).

Estimation of per-acre amount with post-stratification— The estimate of $\hat{CWD}_{caS}$ under a post-stratified design using only P3 plots should have a smaller standard error when compared to the unstratified counterpart (0.144). The estimate was 1.833 tons per acre with the standard error equal to 0.143 tons per acre, which is only a very slight reduction due to the post-stratification.

Post-stratification applied to the sample that includes the predicted plot values should also exhibit a decrease in the standard error of the estimate. In this case, the estimate was 1.686 tons per acre with a standard error of 0.115 tons per acre. Again, the post-stratification had little effect in reducing the standard error of per-acre estimates.

Discussion

Although the differences in means between the observed (P3) and predicted values (P2) were not statistically different at the 95 percent confidence level, the slightly larger mean value of CWD_c from the P3 plots (table 5.5) resulted in estimates of population total CWD_c being slightly larger when compared to the estimates from P2 plots (fig. 5.2). Given the spatial balance of the sample, the smaller mean associated with the predicted values for P2 plots likely arises due to less standing dead biomass, on average, on P2 plots than on P3 plots. The narrower confidence interval for the P2 plots reflects the additional information gained by prediction of CWD_c for plots where it was not sampled. The standard error of the estimates was reduced roughly 20 percent due to the use of the regression model. Although the P3 and P2 estimates are not entirely independent, i.e., the P3 plots are a subset of P2, the wide range of overlap of the confidence intervals suggests the differences in the estimates are statistically nonsignificant.

Similar results were obtained for estimates of $\hat{CWD}_{ca}$ (fig. 5.3). The differences between the P3 and P2 estimates arise from both the differences in $\hat{CWD}_c$ and differences in estimates of area of forest land $\hat{F}$. The estimated forest land from P3 was 18,728,345 acre, while the P2 estimate was 19,146,841 acres. Thus, $\hat{CWD}_c$ from P2 had to be distributed over a larger number of acres. Again, the large amount of overlap suggests the estimates are not statistically different.

Post-stratification resulted in $\hat{CWD}_{cS}$ being slightly larger than $\hat{CWD}_c$ due to all plots not receiving exactly the same weight (fig. 5.2). The post-stratification did improve the precision of the estimates, as the standard errors were reduced by about 10 percent. Overall, the most precise estimates were obtained from the P2 sample with stratification. The P2 estimate without stratification was more precise than the P3 estimate with stratification, indicating that prediction of missing values on P2 plots is more advantageous than post-stratifying P3 plots.

Post-stratification had little impact on the precision of $\hat{CWD}_{caS}$ (fig. 5.3). For both the P3 and P2 samples, applying post-stratification had virtually no effect on the standard error (reduction of <1 percent). The resultant smaller estimator variances $V(\hat{F}_S)$ and $V(\hat{CWD}_{cS})$ were offset by a concomitant decrease in $Cov(\hat{CWD}_{cS}, \hat{F}_S)$ such that the precision of the per-acre estimate remained essentially unchanged. Thus, increased precision of $\hat{CWD}_{caS}$ derives almost entirely from the use of the regression model and no advantage is obtained via post-stratification.

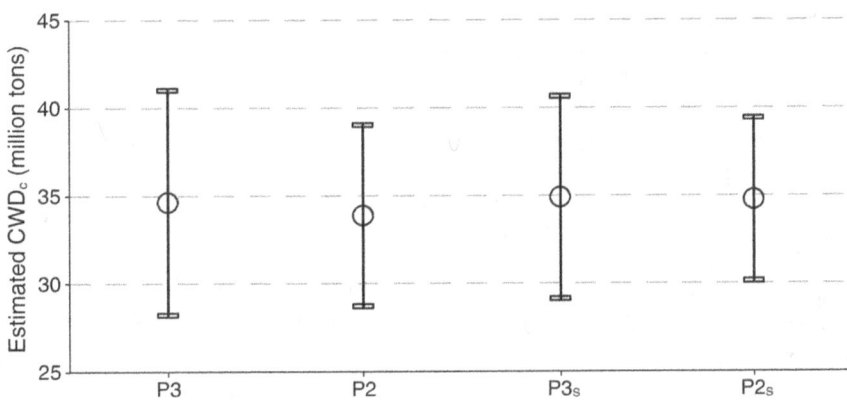

Figure 5.2—Estimates and 95 percent confidence intervals for $\hat{CWD}_c$ using P3 plots, using P2 plots with CWD_c predicted from the ZIG regression model, and these same estimates using post-stratification (P3$_s$, P2$_s$).

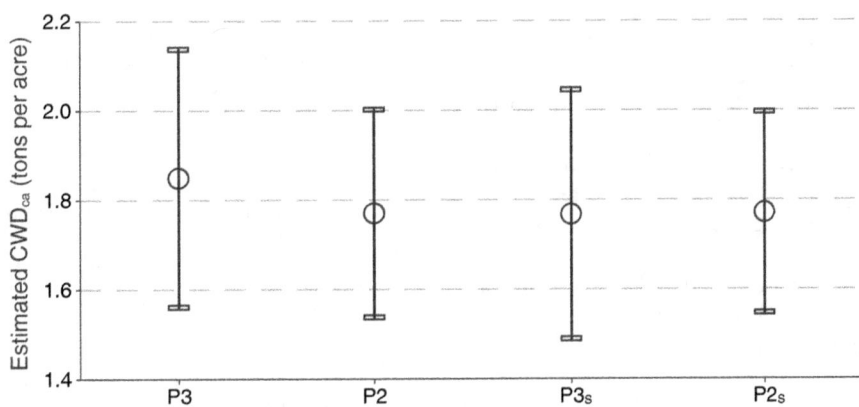

Figure 5.3—Estimates and 95 percent confidence intervals for $\hat{CWD}_{ca}$ using P3 plots, using P2 plots with CWD_c predicted from the ZIG regression model, and these same estimates using post-stratification (P3$_s$, P2$_s$).

Increasing the precision of estimates requires new information that almost always comes at some cost. In the context of this paper, new information could be gained through 1) sampling more plots for CWD_c, 2) developing a regression model for unsampled plots, and/or 3) implementation of post-stratification. All of these options require additional commitments of personnel and equipment. A good starting point for analyzing cost/benefit scenarios is to compute the number of sample plots needed to match the precision obtained via other methods. For instance, the results indicate that the effective sample size for $\hat{CWD}_{cs}$ using the regression model and post-stratification would be 722 plots. This would be 341 more plots in addition to the 381 already being sampled—essentially a doubling of the data collection effort. Similarly, the use of the regression model alone to

obtain $\hat{CWD}_c$ provides an effective sample size of 584 sampled plots (203 additional plots). Having estimates of operating expenses for the various options will allow managers to assess which methods are likely to be the most cost effective.

A number of factors must be considered in such an evaluation. First, one must ascertain the actual cost of collecting the attribute of interest. If this attribute is the only data being collected on sample plots, then all costs must be considered (salary, vehicles, equipment, etc.). However, if a number of other attributes are being collected, the cost is primarily salary (time) as the field crew would be sampling that plot anyway, and opportunity costs as the field crew could be doing something else during that time. Second, one must have a reasonable approximation of the strength of correlations between model input variables and the response variable, and the amount of time needed to develop the relationships. As shown in figure 5.1, the model R^2 has a substantial effect on reduction of the standard error (and the associated effective sample size). Third, costs involved in post-stratification work also need to be assessed. Again, the larger context is important as the costs could be negligible if the post-stratification will be accomplished anyway as part of regular production work (e.g., FIA). Also, peripheral issues such as the value of having observed plot data, e.g., data that may be useful for other purposes besides estimation of population parameters, should also be accounted for in the decision making process.

Conclusion

The use of a regression model to predict values of CWD_c on plots where CWD_c was not assessed had little impact on the estimated values, however, the standard errors of the estimates were reduced about 20 percent. The effectiveness of post-stratification was dependent on the type of estimate. For population total CWD_c, a nearly 10-percent reduction in standard error was obtained. However, for CWD_c per acre of forest land, the post-stratification was ineffective due to offsetting reductions in several terms of the variance estimator. The best results were obtained when using both the regression model and post-stratification for estimates of population total CWD_c, where nearly 27 percent reduction in standard error was achieved.

In the absence of sampling more plots for CWD_c, improvements in the results could be obtained from a better stratification and/or an improved regression model that explains more of the variation in CWD_c (i.e., increase R^2). However, realization of a better result is uncertain as there is no assurance that supplementary allocations of resources will provide improved products. Managers should have reasonable measures for the expected magnitude of improvement vs. costs before undertaking the additional work. If needed improvements in these areas are not forthcoming, then it is likely the best option for increasing precision is to assess CWD_c on more sample plots.

Literature Cited

Balakrishnan, N.; Nevzorov, V.B. 2003. A primer on statistical distributions. Hoboken, NJ: John Wiley. 309 p.

Chojnacky, D.C.; Mickler , R.A.; Heath , L.S.; Woodall, C.W. 2004. Estimates of down woody materials in Eastern U.S. forests. Environmental Management. 33, Suppl. 1: S44–S55.

Coble, D.W; Grogan, J. 2007. Comparison of systematic line-point and double sampling designs for pine and hardwood forests in the Western Gulf. Southern Journal of Applied Forestry. 31(4): 199–206.

Cochran, W.G. 1977. Sampling Techniques, 3rd ed. New York: John Wiley. 428 p.

Coulston, J.W. 2008. Forest inventory and stratified estimation: A cautionary note. Res. Note SRS–16. Asheville, NC: U.S. Department of Agriculture Forest Service, Southern Research Station. 8 p.

El-Shaarawi, A.H.; Piegorsch, W.W., eds. 2002. Encyclopedia of environmetrics. West Sussex, England: John Wiley. 2,672 p.

Feuerverger, A. 1979. On some methods of analysis for weather experiments. Biometrika. 66: 655–658.

Gillis, M.D. 2001. Canada's national forest inventory (responding to current information needs). Environmental Monitoring and Assessment. 67:121–129.

Kangas A.; Maltamo, M., eds. 2006. Forest inventory: methodology and applications. Netherlands: Springer. 362 p.

Katila, M.; Heikkinen, J.; Tomppo, E. 2000. Calibration of small-area estimates for map errors in multisource forest inventory. Canadian Journal of Forest Research. 30: 1329–1339.

Khan, S.; Tripathi, J.P. 1967. The use of multivariate auxiliary information in double sampling. Journal of Indian Statistical Association. 5: 42–48.

Köhl, M. 2001. Methods: inventory concept NF12. In: Brassel, P.; Lischke, H., eds. Swiss national forest inventory: methods and models of the second assessment. Birmensdorf, Switzerland: WSL Swiss Federal Research Institute. 336 p.

Nilsson, M.; Holm, S.; Reese, H. [and others]. 2005. Improved forest statistics from the swedish national forest inventory by combining field data and optical satellite data using post-stratification. In: Proceedings, EARSel, IUFRO, ISPRS workshop ForestSAT 2005. Swedish Forest Agency: Report 8a. 22–26.

Reams, G.A.; Smith, W.D.; Hansen, M.H. [and others]. 2005. The forest inventory and analysis sampling frame. In: Bechtold, W.A.; Patterson, P.L., eds. The enhanced forest inventory and analysis program— national sampling design and estimation procedures. Gen. Tech. Rep. SRS–80. Asheville, NC: U.S. Department of Agriculture Forest Service, Southern Research Station. 11–26.

Scott, C.T.; Bechtold, W.A.; Reams, G.A. [and others]. 2005. Sample-based estimators used by the forest inventory and analysis national information management system. In: Bechtold, W.A.; Patterson, P.L., eds. The enhanced forest inventory and analysis program—national sampling design and estimation procedures. Gen. Tech. Rep. SRS–80. Asheville, NC; U.S. Department of Agriculture Forest Service, Southern Research Station. 43–67.

Schreuder, H.T.; Gregoire, T.G.; Wood, G.B. 1993. Sampling methods for multiresource forest inventory. New York: John Wiley. 464 p.

Chapter 6: Coarse Woody Debris Carbon Estimation Using Nearest Neighbor Methods

Christopher Woodall, Barry Wilson, and James Westfall

Introduction

Although phase 3 (P3) attributes, such as stand coarse woody debris (CWD) biomass, may be both correlated with and directly modeled from phase 2 (P2) attributes (e.g., standing live tree basal area), there are numerous nonparametric methods that serve as an interesting alternative (Hardle 1989, Altman 1992). Nonparametric methods may predict P3 attributes as a weighted average of the values of neighboring observations. In this process, neighbors are chosen from a database of previously measured observations (known pairs of P2 and P3 attributes). Often these nonparametric methods are referred to as imputation techniques, where values are assigned to observations that lack such data (Van Deusen 1997) (e.g., P3 variables are imputed to P2 plots where P3 data were not collected). Given the relatively sparse sample intensity of P3 plots relative to the diversity of forest ecosystem components they estimate, nonparametric methods may offer several advantages compared to using parametric regression models to predict mean values. First, nonparametric methods may retain the full range of variation of the data as well as the covariance structure of the population (Moeur and Stage 1995), depending upon the number of neighbors used. Second, because P3 estimates would only be chosen from actual P3 measurements taken in the field, no unrealistic predictions can occur, again depending upon the number of neighbors used. This aspect is critical because numerous P3 population estimates are not available for some regions of the country, so inventory analysts lack the ability to identify unrealistic estimates. Finally, P3 estimates could be obtained in all situations where at least some P2/P3 measurements are available. Disadvantages of these non-parametric techniques include requirements of reference material during model development and possibilities of a biased estimator (Altman, 1992). However, given the range of P3 analytical possibilities afforded by nonparametric methods, the techniques of k Nearest Neighbor (kNN), Most Similar Neighbor (MSN), and Gradient Nearest Neighbor (GNN) warrant exploration.

k Nearest Neighbor

The kNN method uses a neighborhood consisting of a constant (k) number of observations, while the size of the neighborhood may vary (for early examples see Tomppo 1990, Nilsson 1997). Additionally, the form of the distance measure (e.g., simple Euclidean distance when assuming uncorrelated predictor dimensions or Mahalanobis distance otherwise) must be specified to define the neighborhood at a given point. The distance measure could be based on simple geographic space or a "space" of stand-level characteristics. For example, if an analyst wanted to estimate the CWD biomass for a P2 plot with 50 ft^2 of basal area, then a neighborhood might be defined as k = 3 where 3 P2/P3 plots would be chosen that have a basal area closest to 50 ft^2. In order to reduce the possibility of estimator bias, measurements of CWD biomass could be weighted by their distance from the 50 ft^2 basal area in the kNN estimator. The kNN technique is often used to estimate values for multiple forest variables for georeferenced raster pixels that were not sampled with a field plot. In such cases, values for these variables are estimated for unsampled pixels by computing the weighted average of k nearby field plots, where proximity is based on the specified distance measure as applied to the space defined by the predictor variables, typically called the featurespace. In such applications, the predictor variables typically include data derived from satellite imagery (e.g., spectral data) or other raster data sources. Often, plot weights are chosen to be inversely proportional to their distances in the predictor featurespace. To date, the kNN technique has been demonstrated to be rapid, cost-effective, and accurate when used in national-scale multi-resource inventories (for examples see Franco-Lopez and others 2001; McRoberts and others 2002; Haapanen and others 2004).

Most Similar Neighbor

The MSN method is closely related to the kNN technique. The major difference is that MSN uses canonical correlation analysis to determine distance function (Moeur and Stage 1995, Moeur and Riemann Hershey 1999). While the MSN was designed to use only one neighbor, larger numbers of neighbors can be used to define the neighborhood. We will denote using the canonical correlation technique to create neighborhoods larger than one observation as kMSN. A primary advantage of MSN is that all possible independent (e.g., P2 basal area) and dependent (e.g., CWD biomass) variables can be used in the calculation of canonical correlation (i.e., accommodation of a multivariate response variable). A possible disadvantage is that canonical correlation analysis assumes a linear response function and can perform poorly when forest attributes exhibit a nonlinear response across long gradients (Ohmann and Gregory 2002). Using P2/P3 data as an example, canonical correlation analysis may be used to develop a linear model between P2 live-tree basal area and P3 CWD biomass. This model would in turn be used to weight the P3 observations during the imputation process.

Gradient Nearest Neighbor

The GNN method was first developed by Ohmann and Gregory (2002) for producing spatially explicit vegetation maps by utilizing direct gradient analysis and nearest-neighbor imputation to assign detailed ground-forest attributes to every pixel in a map. Ohmann and Gregory (2002) describe several steps in order to conduct GNN. First, direct gradient analysis is conducted using stepwise canonical correspondence analysis (CCA) (ter Braak 1986, ter Braak and Prentice 1988) to develop a model that quantifies relations between ground (response) data and mapped (explanatory) data. Unlike canonical correlation analysis, CCA does not assume a linear response function. Second, scores are predicted for CCA axes for each pixel by applying coefficients from the model developed in step 1 to the mapped values for explanatory variables. Third, for each mapped pixel a single plot that is nearest in CCA axes dimensional gradient space (distance is Euclidean and axis scores are weighted by their eigenvalues). Finally, ground attributes of the nearest-neighbor plot are imputed to the mapped pixel. However, in some variants of the GNN methodology, more than one neighbor is used with weightings similar to kNN, which we will call kGNN.

Methods

Data

In order to illustrate the application of nearest neighbor methods for the mapping and estimation of P3 attributes, we utilized the study dataset described in the introduction. Briefly, the dataset consists of 381 P3 plots sampled across Michigan forest land (2002–06) for CWD with application of decay reduction and carbon density factors to produce an estimate of CWD carbon (CWDc, tons per acre) for each plot. A suite of geospatial data for the entire study area was acquired and resampled to a pixel resolution of 250 meters: MOD13Q vegetation index data derived from Moderate Resolution Imaging Spectroradiometer imagery collected from 2001–06, climate data from the Daymet database, topographic data from the Elevation Derivatives for National Applications database, and Omernik's ecoregions. Estimates of CWDc were only available on a sparse P3 plot intensity collected by Forest Inventory and Analysis (FIA) from 2002–06.

Analysis

kGNN was used to illustrate the technique of assigning field data values to pixels in a raster dataset. A CCA model was developed that related the geospatial predictor data to the field plot values of interest. The coefficients estimated from the model were used to transform the geospatial predictor data into a small set of CCA axes (i.e., canonical variates), thereby defining a featurespace wherein nearest neighbors could be found using Euclidean distance. In this way, every pixel in the geospatial dataset was assigned a value for the field attribute of interest (CWD_c), by finding the nearest k pixels in the CCA featurespace that also contained field plots and computing a weighted mean of the k corresponding field values.

The assignment of imputed values to pixels creates a new opportunity for estimation of the total CWD_c in the population. Instead of employing classical estimation methods using the observed data on the 381 P3 plots, the data points from all pixels can be utilized to take advantage of the auxiliary information provided by the remotely-sensed image. While various kNN estimation techniques have been proposed in the scientific literature, we chose to use the design-based procedures described by Baffetta and others (2009) to illustrate general concepts. The proposed estimators for the population total and associated variance are respectively:

$$\hat{CWD}_c \quad A_T \left[\sum_{j=1}^{N} \tilde{y}_j + \sum_{j=1}^{n} \frac{y_j \quad \tilde{y}_j}{\pi_j} \right]$$

$$V\left(\hat{CWD}_c\right) \quad A_T^2 \left[\frac{1}{n(n \quad 1)} \sum_{j=1}^{n} \left(\frac{n(y_j \quad \tilde{y}_j)}{N\pi_j} \right. \right.$$
$$\left. \left. \frac{1}{N} \sum_{j=1}^{n} \frac{y_j \quad \tilde{y}_j}{\pi_j} \right)^2 \right]$$

where:

$\hat{CWD}_c$ = estimated population total coarse woody carbon
y_j = CWD_c for pixel j observed at the plot level
$\tilde{y}_j$ = kNN-imputed CWD_c for pixel j
π_j = inclusion probability for pixel j
N = number of pixels in population
n = number of sample plots in population
A_T = area of population

The FIA sample design uses a hexagonal grid to spatially distribute sample plots (Reams and others 2005). As such, the design fits into the one-point stratified paradigm as described by Baffeta and others (2009). While this feature has implications for joint inclusion probabilities for pixels, the first-order inclusion probabilities are the same as those of a random sample ($\pi_j = n/N$). To evaluate any effects due to the value of k, estimates were calculated for values of k = 1, 3, 5, 10, 15, 20, 25, and 30. Standard errors for the estimates were calculated as the square root of the variance.

Results/Discussion

For comparative purposes, estimates were computed assuming simple random sampling using only the 381 P3 plots that were sampled for CWD_c. The estimated total CWD_c for Michigan was 34,628,709 tons with a standard error of 3,199,258 tons. Using the kGNN estimation procedure described above to determine the values assigned to each pixel, estimates for the 8 values of k were calculated (table 6.1). The estimates from the kGNN imputation procedure were slightly less than the estimate obtained from the observed data under a simple random sample design. However, these deviations were quite small; all being in the range of -1.1 to -1.6 percent over the range of k values. To put these differences in context, sampling error ranged from 8.7 to 10.4 percent. Thus, the kGNN estimates are not statistically different from those obtained from the observed P3 plots.

The standard errors for estimates using k = 1 and k = 3 are larger than the standard error using only the observed data (table 6.1), which may be a function of this study's selected estimator in contrast to design-based inference. Standard errors for estimates using k ≥5 were smaller than found with only P3 plots and standard errors decreased as k increased. For k = 30, there was nearly a 6.5 percent reduction in

standard error as compared to the P3 sample. However, it was also notable that relatively small reductions in standard error were achieved beyond k = 15. Using k = 15, reasonable wall-to-wall estimates of CWD_c may be provided for a region (fig. 6.1). For k >3, standard errors may be reduced due to the additional information obtained from the auxiliary data with a "point of diminishing returns" as k exceeds 15. Analysts will need to balance the diminishing reductions in standard errors with longer data processing times due to increasing k.

How do CWD_c estimates derived from the kGNN imputation method compare to simulated CWD_c stocks? In the past, the U.S. used a model Carbon Calculation Tool, (CCT) to simulate CWD_c stocks in forests due to the unavailability of downed-deadwood field data (Smith and others 2007, Woodall and others 2008). The CCT estimates downed deadwood carbon as a function of stand age, forest type, and live-tree stocking. The CCT modeled (Smith and others 2007) estimate of downed deadwood carbon was 47,490,809 tons of carbon for Michigan 2002–06, compared to the GNN (k = 15) and simple random sampling estimates of 34,628,709 and 34,248,000 tons, respectively. As found with comparing CCT estimates of standing dead to P2 estimates (Woodall and others 2012), there can be many sources of estimate divergence, not the least being discrepancies in population definitions. CCT estimates of downed deadwood carbon include medium and large fine woody debris (transect diameter between 1 and 3 inches) while the kGNN exercise in this study solely considered CWD. However, fine woody debris stocks are generally minimal compared to CWD_c at the latitudes of Michigan (Woodall and Liknes 2008). Discrepancies between predicted values of CWD_c, derived from models and those derived from the kGNN imputation procedure will need to be further evaluated and refined across regions and forest conditions.

Conclusion

Nearest neighbor techniques may afford the opportunity to produce landscape-level coverage of forest health indicators to inform both landscape-scale monitoring efforts and stand-level forest health dynamics research. Given the tremendous investment in effort to measure indicators of forest health on a few thousand plots across the Nation, coupling these field data with extensive geospatial datasets using nearest neighbor modeling techniques may be advantageous. Although the sparse sampling intensity of forest health plots across the nation may lack the certainty to inform local efforts to assess and manage local-scale forest health issues, the use of nearest-neighbor modeling techniques (e.g., GNN) may leverage field data utility to benefit policy makers and scientists alike.

Table 6.1—Estimates of CWD_c, standard error of CWD_c, and percent sampling error at various levels of k

k	CWD_c	Standard error	SE
	- - - - - - tons - - - - - -		%
1	34,082,396	3,551,683	10.4
3	34,141,254	3,233,493	9.5
5	34,132,243	3,107,527	9.1
10	34,155,197	3,044,554	8.9
15	34,226,292	3,011,393	8.8
20	34,248,655	3,008,447	8.8
25	34,247,669	2,999,024	8.8
30	34,221,011	2,992,505	8.7

CWD_c = coarse woody debris carbon, k = number of nearest neighbors; SE = sampling error.

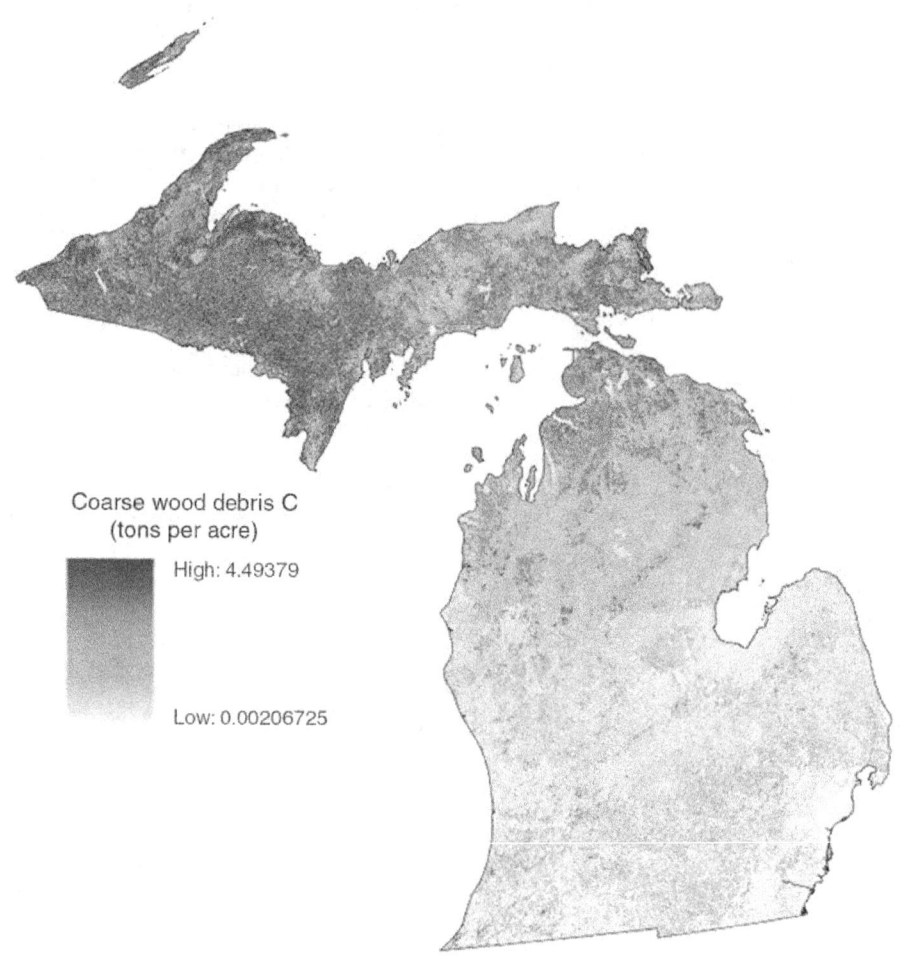

**Coarse wood debris C
(tons per acre)**

High: 4.49379

Low: 0.00206725

Figure 6.1—Estimates of coarse woody debris carbon (CWD$_c$, tons per acre) using nearest neighbor imputation of P3 field plot values of CWD$_c$ to each 250m pixel using Euclidean distance in a canonical correspondence featurespace to measure proximity, with inverse distance weighting of plot values (k = 15), Michigan, 2002–06.

Literature Cited

Altman, N.S. 1992. An introduction to kernel and nearest-neighbor nonparametric regression. The American Statistician. 46: 175–185.

Baffetta, F.; Fattorini, L.; Franceschi, S.; Corona, P. 2009. Design-based approach to k-nearest neighbours technique for coupling field and remotely sensed data in forest surveys. Remote Sensing of Environment. 113: 463–475.

Franco-Lopez, H.; Ek, A.R.; Bauer, M.E. 2001. Estimation and mapping of forest stand density, volume, and cover type using the k-nearest neighbors method. Remote Sensing of Environment. 37: 35–46.

Haapanen, R.; Ek, A.R.; Bauer, M.E.; Finley, A.O. 2004. Delineation of forest/non-forest and other land-use/cover classes using k nearest neighbor classification. Remote Sensing of the Environment. 89: 265–271.

Hardle, W. 1989. Applied nonparametric regression. United Kingdom: Cambridge University Press. 323 p.

McRoberts, R.E.; Nelson, M.D.; Wendt, D.G. 2002. Stratified estimation of forest area using satellite imagery, inventory data, and the k-nearest neighbors technique. Remote Sensing of the Environment. 82: 457–468.

Moeur, M.; Riemann Hershey, R. 1999. Preserving spatial and attribute correlation in the interpolation of forest inventory data. In: Lowell, K.; Jaton, A., eds. Spatial accuracy assessment: land information uncertainty in natural resources. Chelsea, MI: Ann Arbor Press: 419–430.

Moeur, M.; Stage, A.R. 1995. Most similar neighbor: an improved sampling inference procedure for natural resource planning. Forest Science. 41: 337–359.

Nilsson, M. 1997. Estimation of forest variables using satellite image data and airborne lidar. Swedish University of Agricultural Sciences. Umea, Sweden: Ph.D. thesis. [Pages unknown].

Ohmann, J.L.; Gregory, M.J. 2002. Predictive mapping of forest composition and structure with direct gradient analysis and nearest-neighbor imputation in Coastal Oregon, U.S.A. Canadian Journal of Forest Research. 32: 725–741.

Reams, G.A.; Smith, W.D.; Hansen, M.H. [and others]. 2005. The Forest Inventory and Analysis sampling frame. In: Bechtold, W.A.; Patterson, P.L., eds. The enhanced forest inventory and analysis program—national sampling design and estimation procedures. Gen. Tech. Rep. SRS–80, Asheville, NC: U.S. Department of Agriculture Forest Service, Southern Research Station. 11–26.

Smith, J.E.; Heath, L.S.; Nichols, M.C. 2007. U.S. forest carbon calculation tool: forest land carbon stocks and net annual stock change. Gen. Tech. Rep. NRS–13. Newtown Square, PA: U.S. Department of Agriculture Forest Service, Northern Research Station. [CD-ROM].

ter Braak, C.J.F. 1986. Canonical correspondence analysis: a new eigenvector technique for multivariate direct gradient analysis. Ecology. 67: 1167–1179.

ter Braak, C.J.F.; Prentice, J.C. 1988. A theory of gradient analysis. Advances in Ecology Research. 18: 271–313.

Tomppo, E. 1990. Designing a satellite image-aided national forest survey in Finland. In: Proceedings of the SNS/IUFRO workshop on the usability of remote sensing for forest inventory and planning. Umea, Sweden: International Union of Forest Research Organizations, Vienna: 43–47.

Van Deusen, P.C. 1997. Annual forest inventory statistical concepts with emphasis on multiple imputation. Canadian Journal of Forestry Research. 27: 379–384.

Woodall, C.W.; Heath, L.S.; Smith, J.E. 2008. National inventories of down dead woody material forest carbon stocks in the United States: challenges and opportunities. Forest Ecology and Management. 256: 221–228.

Woodall, C.W.; Domke, G.M.; MacFarlane, D.W.; Oswalt, C.M. 2012. Comparing field- and model-based standing dead tree carbon stock estimates across forests of the United States. Forestry. 85: 125–133.

Woodall, C.W.; Liknes, G.C. 2008. Climatic regions as an indicator of forest coarse and fine woody debris carbon stocks in the United States. Carbon Balance and Management. 3: 5.

Chapter 7: Overview of Data Mining Approaches

David Gartner

Introduction

It is not within the scope of this publication to determine the best method for analyzing the relationship between the phase 2 (P2) data and the phase 3 (P3) data for each of the P3 variables. That task is larger than can be handled in a chapter or even in a single publication. The methods mentioned in this chapter are not specifically designed for the relationships between P2 and P3 variables and should be considered merely as suggestions. Nor is this chapter designed to give detailed instructions on any of the data mining techniques, but rather give an overview of some of the methods currently available.

Most classical statistical methods have been designed using relatively small datasets and simple models, such as simple linear regression. As computing power increased, more complex methods such as nonlinear regression have been developed. Nonlinear regression required having knowledge of the shape of the expected relationship. This knowledge allowed calculating predictive equations with relatively small datasets. As computing power continued to increase, methods for creating predictive equations assuming no prior relationships between the independent and dependent variables (data mining methods) were created. These methods usually depend on generating a large number of trial parameters (regression parameters or splitting points) and then selecting a small subset. Because of this large number of trial parameters, the data mining methods are susceptible to overfitting the data. Therefore, data mining methods are used on large datasets (>1,000 observations) with relatively low expected coefficients of determination ($R^2 < 0.2$). These methods include: self-organizing maps, neural networks, classification and regression trees, random forests, and bagging trees.

Besides requiring large datasets, data mining techniques often include other methods to help avoid overfitting. These methods consist of splitting the dataset into parts, using one part to fit the model and the other part to determine how well the model performed. One version uses one relatively large portion of the dataset (30–50 percent), called a holdout or validation dataset, to determine how well the model performed. The other version is to repeatedly resample the dataset to determine how well the model performed. The two main methods for resampling are 1) repeatedly drawing full-sized datasets from the original dataset using sampling with replacement, called bootstrapping (Efron 1979), or 2) by dividing the dataset into equal-sized subsets and leaving one subset out each time, called cross-validation.

Five different data mining methods are examined in this section: self-organizing maps, neural networks, Classification And Regression Trees (CART), bagging trees (bootstrap aggregating), and Random Forests. Self-organizing maps and neural networks are closely related. Bagging trees and Random Forests are actually modifications of CART. The dataset will be split into a training dataset of 173 observations used to fit each method, and a holdout dataset of 75 observations used to determine how well the predictions match observed data for each method. The same training dataset and test dataset will be used for all five methods. The predictor variables from the segmented linear regression analysis in chapter 3 will be used: stand age, latitude, harvesting, dead-tree volume, live-tree volume, and indictor variables for mesic and hydric soil conditions. To ensure that the same data are used with each analysis method, and to avoid quirks of some of the software, the data for each variable were scaled to the range [0,1] by dividing by the maximum observed value.

Self-Organizing Maps

The intent of self-organizing maps is to organize observations into groups with similar values along two latent environmental axes (Kohonen 1982). It comes in two main forms: unsupervised and supervised. For unsupervised self-organizing maps, the algorithm starts with a grid consisting usually of squares or hexagons to which a small subset of the observations is assigned. The other observations are then placed in the cell with the most similar observation. Then the cell centers are modified based on the observations in that cell and in the cells in the area around it. Initially, the area of other cells considered is fairly large, which forces the most dissimilar observations to opposite ends of the environmental axes. As the area of other cells being considered when creating new cell centers is decreased, observations with intermediate dissimilarities end up placed in cells along the gradient of the latent environmental variable. The end result is a merger of cluster analysis and indirect gradient analysis. A final cluster analysis on the cells is possible, if a cluster analysis is the final objective. This would lead to the possibility of making not only a map of the clusters, but also maps of the original variables. Comparing the two sets of maps will give the user a better understanding of the variables that are driving the formation of the clusters than standard cluster analysis.

For supervised self-organizing maps (Melssen and others 2006), the process is the same except that the cells for the predictor variables are based on observations with similar values of the target variables. The final maps will have cells with different levels of the target variable and maps of the same cells with the mean value of the predictor variables for the same cells. While the cluster analysis capabilities of unsupervised self-organizing maps may be of interest to the users, this publication is specifically about exploring the relationship between P2 and P3 variables. Therefore, only the supervised version of the self-organizing maps will be demonstrated here.

Example of Self-Organizing Maps using the Coarse Woody Debris Carbon Data

The bidirectional Kohonen routine from the R package 'kohonen' (Wehrens 2012) was used to generate a supervised self-organizing map. A 5 x 4 hexagonal grid was used. First the training dataset was used to fit the map. Then the resulting map was examined for new information about the relationship between the P2 and coarse woody debris carbon (CWD_c). Then the holdout dataset was used to determine how well the map would predict new data.

The map is displayed in figures 7.1A–7.1H. The cell with the highest amount of CWD_c is in the lower right-hand corner, with the two closest cells having intermediate CWD_c values. After those cells the amount of CWD_c drops off fairly quickly. The map layers for stand age, harvesting, latitude, mesic soils, and hydric soils don't show clear relationships between the P2 variables and CWD_c. The cell with the highest mean dead-tree volume is one of the cells with the intermediate CWD_c, and the cell with the second most dead-tree volume matches the cell with the most CWD_c. This shows that while there is a relationship between dead-tree volume and CWD_c, the strength of the relationship is limited. The cell with the largest mean live-tree volume is in the same cell as the largest mean CWD_c. However within the cells with lower levels of live-tree volume, the relationship disappears. This suggests the possibility that above a certain level of live-tree volume, there is a relationship between live-tree volume and CWD_c, but below that level of live-tree volume any relationship between live tree volume and CWD_c gets lost in the noise.

To determine how well the map was at predicting new data, the holdout dataset target variable values were predicted using the fitted map and the holdout dataset's predictor variables values (fig. 7.2). Then the sum squared differences between the observed and the predicted values were compared to the sum squared differences between the observed values and the training dataset target variable mean and the holdout dataset target variable mean. The

sum of squares for the holdout dataset mean is 1.409, the sum of squares of the training dataset mean is 1.414, and the sum of squares for the self-organized map predictions is 1.718. Therefore, this map does not predict the holdout dataset well. This is probably due to the large amount of variability in the CWD_c data.

Examples of Self-Organizing Maps from the Literature

Chon (2010) wrote a very good review article of the uses of self-organizing maps in ecological papers. While most of the studies Chon discusses are unsupervised self-organizing maps, Chon talks about supervised self-organizing maps as a direction of future development. Giraudel and Lek (2001) compare unsupervised self-organizing maps with principal components analysis and correspondence analysis. While examples of unsupervised self-organizing maps being used to analyze ecological data: classification of aquatic ecosystems (Park and others 2004), moor and heath vegetation (Foody 1999), and classification of Landsat imagery (Ji 2000); no examples of supervised self-organizing maps were found.

Neural Networks

Neural networks were initially designed for pattern recognition (Bishop 1995). They are designed to mimic the human brain. The basic unit, called a node, uses the levels of the input variables to calculate an output variable (fig. 7.3). Usually the input variables are run through several different nodes, with the output signals being used as input variables into other nodes. A group of nodes drawing input signals from the same variables and sending output signals to the same sets of locations are called a layer (fig. 7.4). A neural network can have any number of nodes and any number of layers. Nodes do not need to connect to all nodes in the next layer.

There are three main types of neural networks: networks with fixed weights, supervised networks which have their weights determined by fitting the model to a target variable, and unsupervised networks which have their weights determined to create relatively homogenous clusters of observations (Giudici 2003). For unsupervised neural networks, the input variables would be the predictor variables like stand age and dead-tree volume, and the output variables would be the cells in a self-organizing map. For supervised neural networks, the input variables would still be the predictor variables, but the output variables would be predictions of target variables, such as CWD_c.

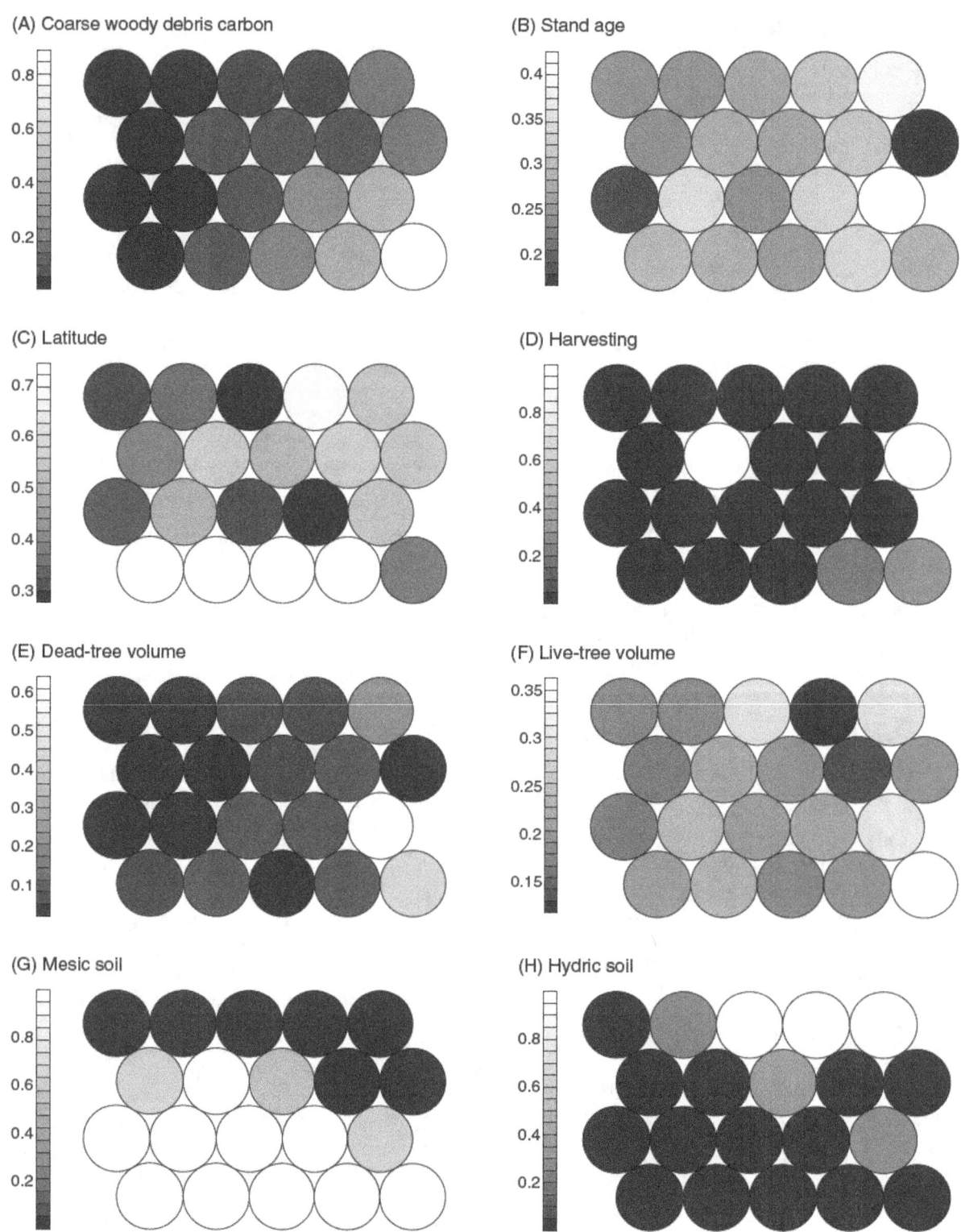

Figure 7.1—Resulting Kohonen bidirectional self-organizing map (A) Coarse woody debris carbon, (B) Stand age, (C) Latitude, (D) Harvesting, (E) Dead-tree volume, (F) Live-tree volume, (G) Mesic soil, and (H) Hydric soil.

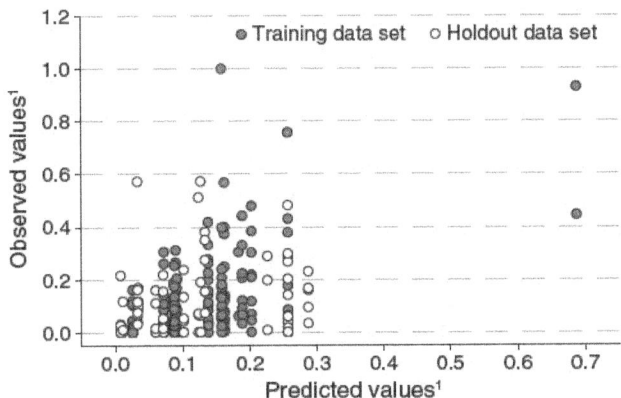

¹Proportion of maximum amount of coarse woody debris carbon per acre.

Figure 7.2—Self-organized map results: observed versus predicted.

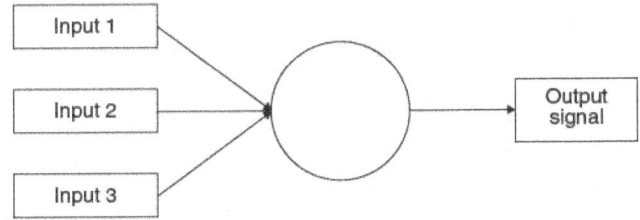

Figure 7.3—Visual example of a node.

Since our objective is to predict the amount of CWD_c on P2 plots from the relationship between P2 variables and the amount of CWD_c on P3 plots, we will be using a supervised network, called a multilayer perceptron. The nodes in the hidden and output layers starts by creating a weighted sum of the input variables with an intercept term, and then performs one of the following functions on the sum to create the output variable. The functions used inside the node to calculate the output signal are 'sigmoid' (logistic function), 'purelin' (linear function), 'hardlim' (step function), and 'tansig' (hyperbolic tangent function) (fig. 7.5). By combining the several nodes in different layers, these node signal equations can approximate complex nonlinear equations. The weights and intercept terms are then estimated by an algorithm that tries to find the combination that creates the best fit between the output values and the target variables. For continuous target variables, the best fit criteria is usually the same minimum sum-squared error used in nonlinear regression. While nonlinear regression algorithms require the user to provide initial parameter estimates, neural network algorithms use a different fitting algorithm that is supposed to be less sensitive to initial parameter estimates to the point that they often use random initial parameter estimates. This flexibility with respect to initial parameter estimates comes at the cost of needing a large dataset.

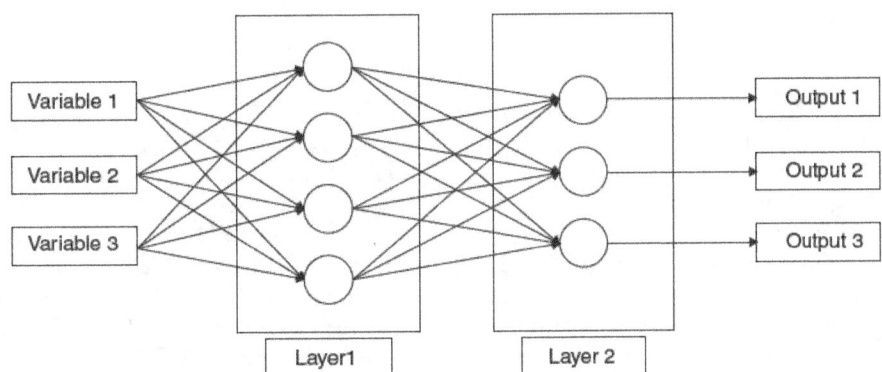

Figure 7.4—Neural network used in example.

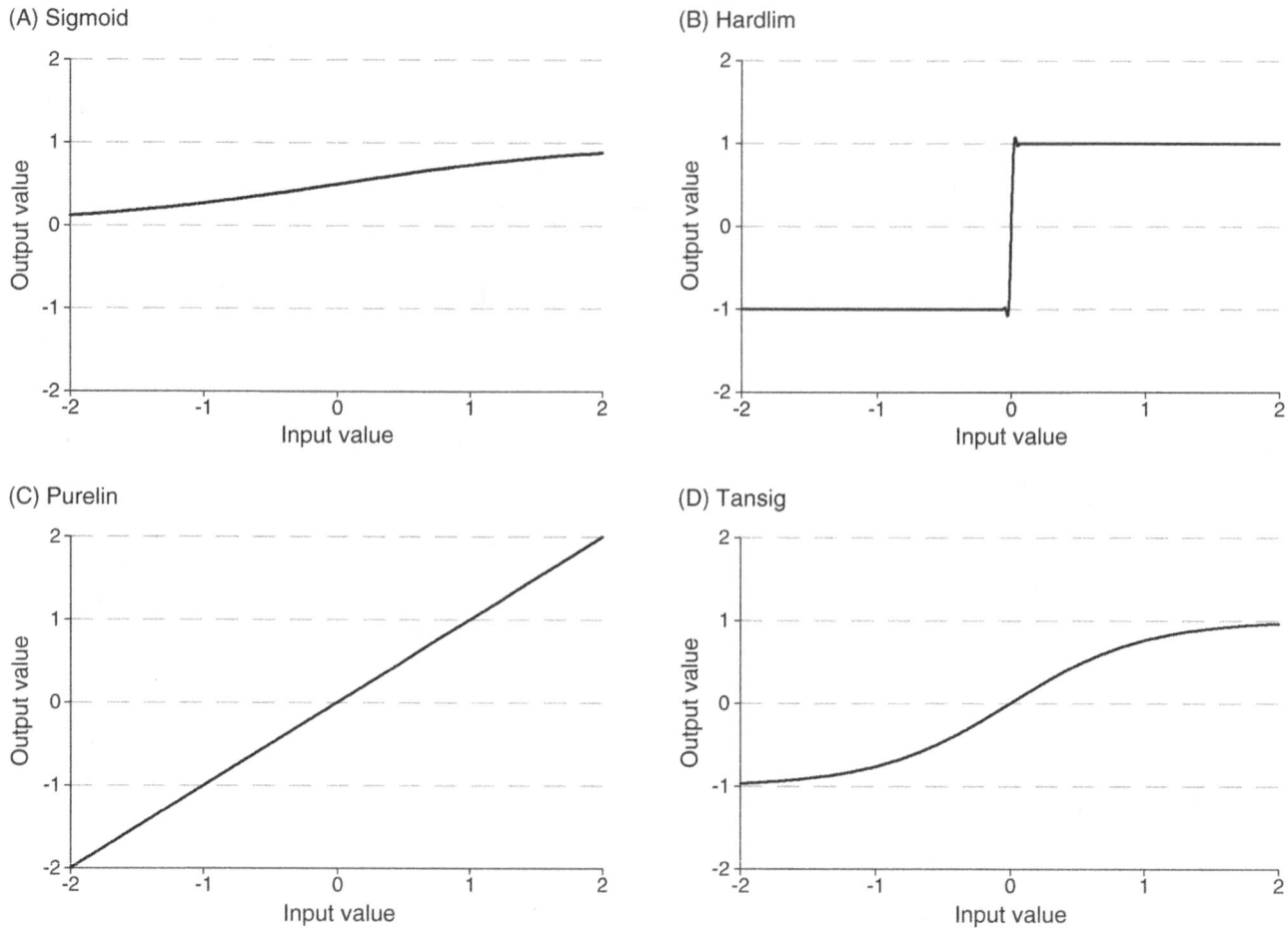

Figure 7.5—Activation functions commonly used in neural networks (A) Sigmoid, (B) Hardlim, (C) Purelin, and (D) Tansig.

Example of Neutral Network Using Coarse Woody Debris Carbon Data

Because we do not have a large number of observations, we will keep our network fairly simple to help prevent overfitting. The main objective in this section is to give the reader a feel for neural networks, as opposed to publishing an actual neural network analysis. We used a neural network with two nodes in a single hidden layer (fig. 7.6). Because there are 7 prediction variable coefficients and 1 intercept term, each of the hidden nodes will contain 8 parameters that need to be estimated, and the output layer node will have 2 input variable coefficients and 1 intercept term for

a total of 19 parameters to be estimated. We analyzed the data run using an R package called 'neuralnet' (Fritsch and Guenther, 2012). This package's input nodes pass the input variables straight through without modification. The hidden nodes used 'sigmoid' functions, with the output node using 'purelin.' The sum-squared error of the training dataset (2.120) is smaller than the sum-squared error around the training set mean (4.275). However, the sum-squared error for the holdout dataset (1.780) is larger than sum-squared error around the training set mean (1.414) suggesting that the model was overfit. The differences in fit for the training and the holdout datasets can be seen in the graph of the observed versus predicted values (fig. 7.7).

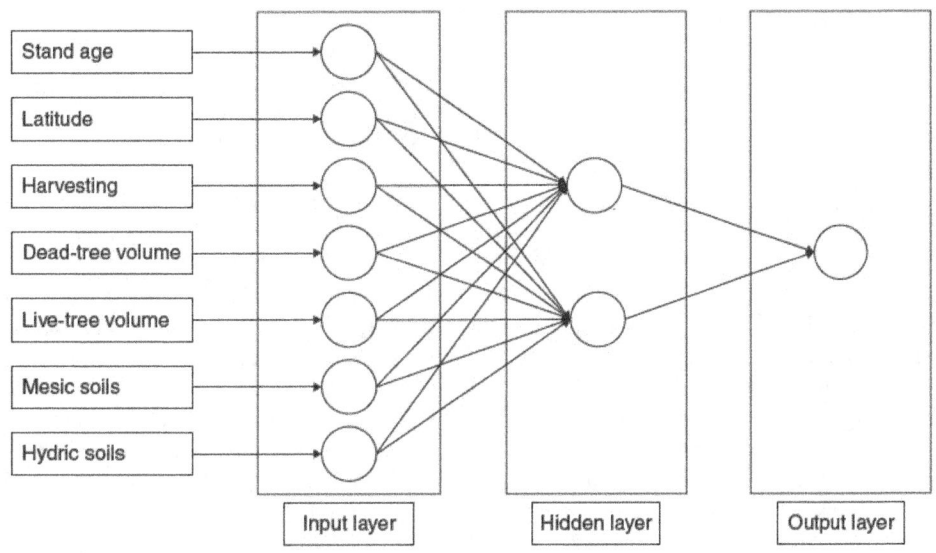

Figure 7.6—Neural network predictions versus the observed CWD$_c$ data.

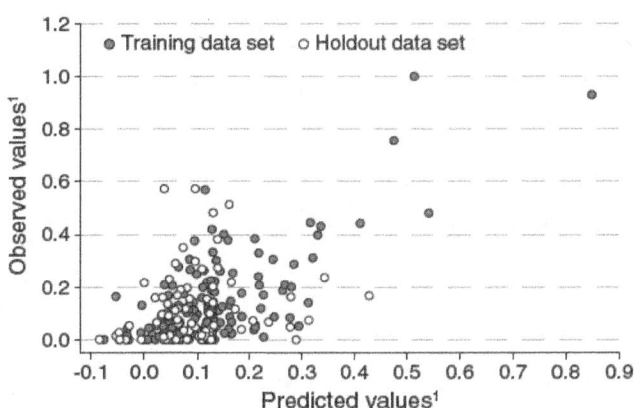

[1]Proportion of maximum amount of coarse woody debris carbon per acre.

Figure 7.7—Neural network results.

Examples of Neutral Networks from the Literature

Neural networks have been used in forest research such as classifying regeneration stages (Kuplich 2006), modeling deforestation (Mas and others 2004), analyzing bird species richness data (Monteil and others 2004), tree-ring data (Zhang and others 2000), and tree survival data (Guan and Gertner 1991). Guan and Gertner (1991) have response surface graphs of some of their neural network models, which may help some people understand the capabilities of neural networks.

Classification And Regression Tree Methods

The original tree method is called Classification And Regression Tree, or CART (Breiman and others 1984). The algorithm for creating a CART takes individual predictor variables and attempts to find the point that splits the data into two or more relatively homogeneous groups. After each split, the process is repeated for each of the subgroups until either a minimum group size is reached, or no split creates more homogeneous groups. The final set of subgroups is often called 'leaves.' The idea is that as the groups become more homogeneous, more of the variation is going to be between groups, and thus explained by the CART. For categorical target variables, the prediction becomes the dominant class in each leaf. For continuous target variables, the prediction becomes the mean of the observations in each leaf.

Bagging trees applies bootstrapping to the observations of a CART to create a set of randomly generated CARTs. Then the results from these CARTs are then averaged together. Random Forests not only randomly samples the observations, but also randomly selects a subset of the prediction variables to be used in each of the individual CARTs. Prasad and others (2006) have written a very good article reviewing and comparing these three methods.

Classification And Regression Tree

The two main methods for making sure that the CART is not overfitting the data is to use either cross-validation or a holdout dataset. Sometimes the dataset is split into three subsets: the first subset is used to create the initial tree, the second subset is used to determine if some of the data splits should be removed, and the third subset is used to determine how well the CART performs.

Example of classification and regression tree using the coarse woody debris carbon data—As an example, we will run a regression tree on the same stand-level CWD$_c$ data as used for the self-organizing map, including the same two subsets: the training and the holdout subset. We used the R package 'tree' (Ripley 2010), with the default minimum of five observations per leaf. The resulting tree (table 7.1) from the training dataset has nine splits using volume of dead trees, harvesting, latitude, stand age, and volume of live trees, but neither of the soil indicator variables was used. When the results of the CART were applied to the holdout dataset, the lowest sum-squared error came from using just the first six splits (table 7.2), which explained about 4.4 percent of the variation. Because the predicted values are the means of seven subgroups, there are only seven different predicted values (fig. 7.8).

Examples of classification and regression trees in the literature—CART has been used to analyzed wildfire data (Brosofske and others 2007), model tree mortality (Dobbertin and Biging 1998), estimate down deadwood (Chojnacky and Heath 2002), analyze harvesting and land-use conversion patterns (McDonald and others 2006), analyze forest bird-habitat relationships (Fearer and others 2007), and help predict locations of populations of a rare herbaceous species (Bourg and others 2005).

Table 7.1—Resulting Classification And Regression Tree

Split number	Node description	Number of observations	SSE	Mean
	Root	173	4.27500	0.12350
1	Dead-tree volume <0.324412	166	2.42100	0.10570
2	Harvesting <0.51	155	1.71700	0.09588
3	Latitude <0.699627	106	0.86730	0.07396
5 y	Dead-tree volume <0.139713	91	0.54140	0.06083
7 x	Age <0.244898	39	0.06923	0.03010
7 x	Age >0.244898	52	0.40770	0.08388
5 x y	Dead-tree volume >0.139713	15	0.21510	0.15360
3	Latitude >0.699627	49	0.68900	0.14330
6 y	Live-tree volume <0.213186	28	0.27360	0.11730
8 x	Age <0.221939	7	0.11130	0.20820
8 x	Age >0.221939	21	0.08507	0.08696
6 y	Live-tree volume >0.213186	21	0.37120	0.17800
9 x	Latitude <0.812949	16	0.14610	0.14060
9 x	Latitude >0.812949	5	0.13140	0.29750
2	Harvesting >0.51	11	0.47940	0.24350
4 x y	Live-tree volume <0.249313	6	0.28800	0.32580
4 x y	Live-tree volume >0.249313	5	0.10210	0.14480
1 x y	Dead-tree volume >0.324412	7	0.54260	0.54760

SSE = sum squared error.

Y denotes end leaf on CART at applying the results of the holdout dataset.

X denotes end leaf on CART created using just the training dataset.

Table 7.2—Comparison between training dataset results and holdout dataset results for classification and regression tree

Split number	Split variable	Training dataset SSE	Holdout dataset SSE
0	All data in one group	100.0000	100.0000
1	Dead volume	69.3188	115.9559
2	Harvest	64.0811	118.1190
3	Latitude	60.3126	102.7378
4	Live volume	58.2237	108.4273
5	Age	55.6303	101.7895
6	Live volume	54.5962	95.6518
7	Age	53.0883	192.0775
8	Age	51.2818	194.6466
9	Latitude	49.0892	198.7355

SSE = sum squared error.

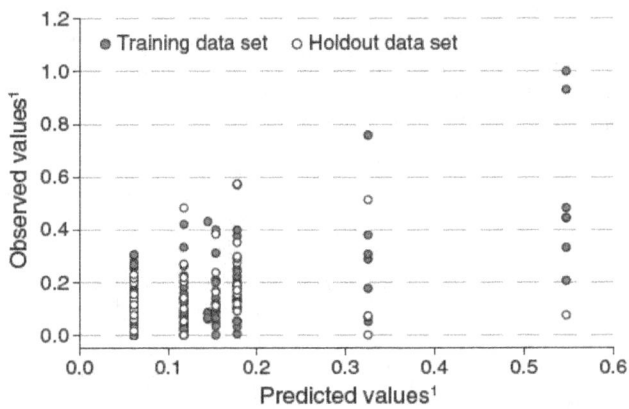

[1]Proportion of maximum amount of coarse woody debris carbon per acre.

Figure 7.8—Classification And Regression Tree results: observed versus predicted.

Bagging Trees

Breiman (1996) created the term *bagging* as an acronym for *bootstrap aggregating*. Bootstrapping creates multiple datasets from the original dataset by sampling the original dataset with replacement. These created sample datasets are then run through the same analysis process as the original dataset. In bagging, the predictions are then aggregated by averaging. In bagging trees, the bootstrap aggregating procedure is applied using CART.

Example of bagging tree using the coarse woody debris carbon data—The R-language bagging tree package 'ipred' (Peters and Hothorn 2009) was used on the same training and holdout datasets used as an example in the CART

section. One hundred randomized trees were used in our example. Because of the averaging of the results from 100 trees, the predicted values are much closer to being continuous than the CART predictions (fig. 7.9). The bagging tree predictions explained 8.8 percent of the variation in the holdout dataset.

Examples of bagging trees in the literature—Most of the examples in the literature are related to analyzing large multivariate datasets such as classification of satellite imagery and other remotely sensed data (Kocev and others 2009, Pal 2008, Briem and others 2002, Tzeng and others 2009) and predicted effects of climate change (Iverson and others 2008, Prasad and others 2006). De'ath (2007) wrote a review of bagging trees, boosted trees, and random forests for ecological modeling.

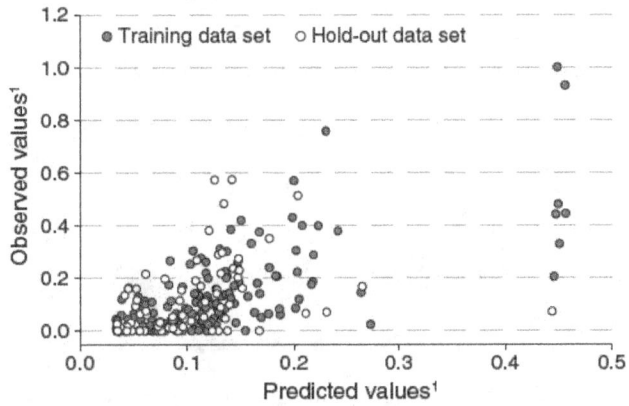

[1]Proportion of maximum amount of coarse woody debris carbon per acre.

Figure 7.9—Bagging tree results: observed versus predicted.

Random Forests

Breiman (2001) took Random Forests one step further beyond bagging trees. At each node of the CART for the resampled datasets, Random Forests selects a random subset of the predictor variables to be used to create the split. This modification is designed especially for datasets with a large number of related predictor variables. The default number of resample datasets is 100. The results of the different trees are then averaged.

Example of Random Forests using coarse woody debris carbon data—Random Forests was run on the same set of training and holdout data used for CART. Using one of the most obvious differences between CART and Random Forests' predictions is that the Random Forests predictions are much closer to continuous than the CART predictions (fig. 7.10). This is due to the way that Random Forests combines the results from the different regression trees. Also, the prediction errors for the holdout dataset are clearly larger than the prediction errors from the training dataset. The mean square error for the holdout dataset is 1.79, while the mean square error for the training dataset is only 0.63. Some of this is due to the small size of the training dataset.

Examples of Random Forests from the literature— Random Forests has been used to predict the effect of climate change on bird ranges (Virkkala and others 2010) and recent aspen mortality (Rehfeldt and others 2009), to analyze factors related to fire severity in the Southwestern United States (Holden and others 2009), and to predict vegetation communities in Belgium (Peters and others 2007).

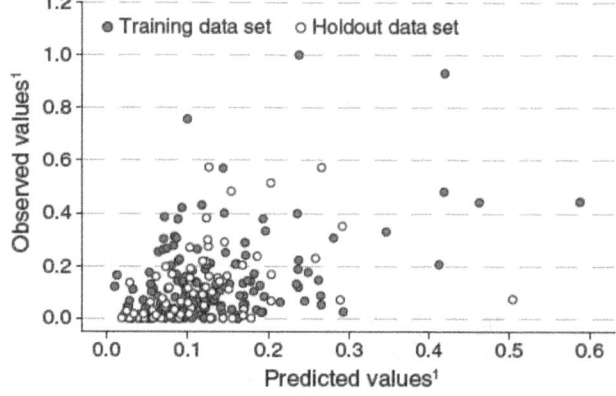

[1]Proportion of maximum amount of coarse woody debris carbon per acre.

Figure 7.10—Random Forests predicted versus observed.

Comments About the Data Mining Methods

There is no method that is best for all analysis. Data mining is evolving quickly, and new methods are created every few years. Therefore, we are not going to make any specific recommendations. For those interested in using data mining techniques for estimating either P3 values on P2 plots or population totals of P3 variables using P2 plot data, we will revisit two issues that arose in chapter 4: estimating P3 values for observations with P2 values outside the range of the training set data and variances.

Extrapolating Beyond the Range of the Training Dataset

Since we found that there are several P2 plots with values of dead-tree volume that are outside the range of values found on the P3 plots (fig. 4.4), we will look at how the different data mining methods will handle these values. Since the predicted values for CARTs are the mean values of observations in the training dataset, the CART predictions of the target variable (CWD_c) has to be within the range of target variable values in the training dataset. This means that, even though there are P2 plots with volume of dead-tree values much larger than those that occur on P3 plots, CART cannot predict a CWD_c value larger than the largest observed value of CWD_c found on a P3 plot. Since bagging trees and Random Forests are the averages of multiple CARTs, these two methods will not make predictions outside the range of the P3 target variable values. Since neural networks essentially create nonlinear equations, their predicted target variable values can be outside the range of values found on P3 plots. How self-organizing maps predict new data outside the range of the training data is unclear. Unfortunately, the only way to tell which method most accurately predicts observations outside the range of the training dataset is to measure some of the observations outside the range of the training dataset, i.e., some of the P2 plots with very large values of dead-tree volumes.

Variances

Deconstructing a CART to determine the variance for each predicted value is not very difficult. The other methods are sufficiently numerically complex that deconstructing them to find the variances to the predicted values is daunting. However, resampling methods similar to those used in bagging trees and Random Forests are capable of creating populations of predictions for each observation to be predicted. Theoretically, this population of predictions could be used to create not only a mean predicted value, but also variance for the predicted value. How the variances for individual predicted values should be incorporated to create variances for predicted values for population totals, such as State totals, has not yet been researched. Because the field of data mining methods is still evolving, the possible methodology may be derived within the next couple of years.

Literature Cited

Bishop, C.M. 1995. Neural networks for pattern recognition. Oxford: Clarendon Press. 504 p.

Briem, G.J.; Benediktsson, J.A.; Sveinsson, J.R. 2002. Multiplie classifiers applied to multisource remote sensing data. IEEE Transactions on Geoscience and Remote Sensing. 40(10): 2291–2299.

Breiman, L. 1996. Bagging predictors. Machine Learning. 24: 123–140.

Breiman, L. 2001. Random forests. Machine Learning. 45: 5–32.

Breiman, L.; Friedman, J.H.; Olshen, R.A.; Stone, C.J. 1984. Classification and regression trees. Florida: CRC Press. 368 p.

Brosofske, K.D.; Cleland, D.T.; Saunders, S.C. 2007. Factors influencing modern wildfire occurrence in the Mark Twain National Forest, Missouri. Southern Journal of Applied Forestry. 31(2): 73–84.

Bourg, N.A.; McShea, W.J.; Gill, D.E. 2005. Putting a CART before the search: successful habitat prediction for a rare forest herb. Ecology. 86(10): 2793–2804.

Chojnacky, D. C.; Heath, L.S. 2002. Estimating down deadwood from FIA forest inventory variables in Maine. Environmental Pollution. 116: S25–S30.

Chon, T.S. 2010. Self-organizing maps applied to ecological sciences. Ecological Informatics. 6: 50–61.

De'ath, G. 2007. Boosted trees for ecological modeling and prediction. Ecology. 88(1): 243–251.

Dobbertin, M.; Biging, G.S. 1998. Using the non-parametric classifier CART to model forest tree mortality. Forest Science. 44(4): 507–516.

Efron, B. 1979. Bootstrap methods: another look at the jackknife. Annals of Statistics. 7(1): 1–26.

Fearer, T.M.; Prisley, S.P.; Stauffer, D.F.; Keyser, P.D. 2007. A method for integrating the breeding bird survey and forest inventory and analysis databases to evaluate forest bird-habitat relationships at multiple spatial scales. Forest Ecology and Management. 243: 128–143.

Foody, G.M. 1999. Applications of the self-organising feature map neural network in community data analysis. Ecological Modelling. 120: 97–107.

Fritsch, S.; Guenther, F. 2012. Package 'neuralnet.' Version 1.31. http://www.r-project.org. [Date accessed unknown].

Giraudel, J.L.; Lek, S. 2001. A comparison of self-organizing map algorithm and some conventional statistical methods for ecological community ordination. Ecological Modelling. 146: 329–339.

Giudici, P. 2003. Applied data mining: statistical methods for business and industry. England: John Wiley. 364 p.

Guan, B.T.; Gertner, G. 1991. Modeling red pine tree survival with an artificial neural network. Forest Science. 37(5): 1429–1440.

Holden, Z.A.; Morgan, P.; Evans, J.S. 2009. A predictive model of burn severity based on 20-year satellite-inferred burn severity data in a large southwestern U.S. wilderness area. Forest Ecology and Management. 258(11): 2399–2406.

Iverson, L.R.; Prasad, A.M.; Matthews, S.N.; Peters, M. 2008. Estimating potential habitat for 134 eastern U.S. tree species under six climate scenarios. Forest Ecology and Management. 254(3): 390–406.

Ji, C.Y. 2000. Land-use classification of remotely sensed data using Kohonen self-organizing feature map neural networks. Photogrammetric Engineering and Remote Sensing. 66(12): 1451–1460.

Kocev, D.; Dzeroski, S.; White, M.D. [and others]. 2009. Using single- and multi-target regression trees and ensembles to model a compound index of vegetation condition. Ecological Modelling. 220(8): 1159–1168.

Kohonen, T. 1982. Self-organized formation of topologically correct feature maps. Biological Cybernetics. 43: 59–69.

Kuplich, T.M. 2006. Classifying regenerating forest stages in Amazonia using remotely sensed images and a neural network. Forest Ecology and Management. 234: 1–9.

Mas, J.F.; Puig, H.; Palacio, J.L.; Sosa-Lopez, A. 2004. Modelling deforestation using GIS and artificial neural networks. Environmental Modelling and Software. 19(5): 461–471.

McDonald, R.I.; Motzkin, G.; Bank, M.S. [and others]. 2006. Forest harvesting and land-use conversion over two decades in Massachusetts. Forest Ecology and Management. 227: 31–41.

Melssen, W.; Wehrens, R.; Buydens, L. 2006. Supervised Kohonen networks for classification problems. Chemometrics and Intelligent Laboratory Systems. 83: 99–13.

Monteil, C.; Deconchat, M.; Balent, G. 2004. Simple neural network reveals unexpected patterns of bird species richness in forest fragments. Landscape Ecology. 20(5): 513–527.

Pal, M. 2008. Ensemble of support vector machines for land cover classification. International Journal of Remote Sensing. 29(10): 3043–3049.

Park, Y.S.; Chon, T.S.; Kwak, I.S.; Lek, S. 2004. Hierarchical community classification and assessment of aquatic ecosystems using artificial neural networks. Science of the Total Environment. 327: 105–122.

Peters, A.; Hothorn, T. 2009. Package 'ipred': improved predictors. Version 0.8-8. http://www.r-project.org. [Date accessed unknown].

Peters, J.; De Baets, B.; Verhoest, N.E.C. [and others]. 2007. Random forests as a tool for ecohydrological distribution modelling. Ecological Modelling. 207: 304–318.

Prasad, A.M.; Iverson, L.R.; Liaw A. 2006. Newer classification and regression tree techniques: bagging and random forests for ecological prediction. Ecosystems. 9: 181–199.

Rehfeldt, G.E.; Ferguson, D.E.; Crookston, N.L. 2009. Aspen, climate, and sudden decline in western USA. Forest Ecology and Management. 258: 2353–2364.

Ripley, B. 2010. Package 'tree.' Version 1.0–28. http://www r-project.org. [Date accessed unknown].

Tzeng, Y.C.; Fan, K.T.; Chen, K.S. 2009, An adaptive thresholding multiple classifiers system for remote sensing image classification. Photogrammetric Engineering and Remote Sensing. 75(6): 679–687.

Virkkala, R.; Marmion, M.; Heikkinen, R.K. [and others]. 2010. Predicting range shifts of northern bird species: influence of modelling technique and topography. Acta Oecologica. 36(3): 269–281.

Wehrens, R. 2012. Package 'kohonen'. Version 2.0.9. http://www r-project. org. [Date accessed unknown].

Zhang, Q.B.; Hebda, R.J.; Zhang, Q.J.; Alfaro, R.I. 2000. Modeling tree-ring growth responses to climatic variables using artificial neural networks. Forest Science. 46(2): 229–239.

Gartner, Dave, Editor. 2013. Use of ancillary data to improve the analysis of forest health indicators. e-Gen. Tech Rep. SRS–179. Asheville, NC: U.S. Department of Agriculture Forest Service, Southern Research Station. 52 p.

In addition to its standard suite of mensuration variables, the Forest Inventory and Analysis (FIA) program of the U.S. Forest Service also collects data on forest health variables formerly measured by the Forest Health Monitoring program. FIA obtains forest health information on a subset of the base sample plots. Due to the sample size differences, the two sets of variables have traditionally been analyzed separately. However, the analysis of forest health indicator data can occur in conjunction with not only other stand characteristics (mensuration variables such as live-tree volume), but also with a plethora of ancillary information such climate data and satellite imagery. This document is designed to help people interested in using auxiliary information in the analysis of the forest health indicators.

Keywords: Analysis, ancillary data, coarse woody debris, estimation, forest health data, FIA.

How do you rate this publication?
Scan this code to submit your feedback
or go to www.srs.fs.usda.gov/pubeval

You may request additional copies of this publication by email at pubrequest@fs.fed.us

www.ingramcontent.com/pod-product-compliance
Lightning Source LLC
Chambersburg PA
CBHW080545290526
45790CB00006B/2556